T0198730

YOU'RE NOT YOUR CAR

A Guide To Finding Peace, Balance,
and Understanding Who You Are
Beyond Your Physical Body

JENNIFER MERRITTS

BALBOA.PRESS
A DIVISION OF HAY HOUSE

Balboa Press books may be ordered through booksellers or by contacting:

Balboa Press
A Division of Hay House
1663 Liberty Drive
Bloomington, IN 47403
www.balboapress.com
844-682-1282

Print information available on the last page.

ISBN: 979-8-7652-3963-6 (sc)
ISBN: 979-8-7652-3965-0 (hc)
ISBN: 979-8-7652-3964-3 (e)

Library of Congress Control Number: 2023903178

Balboa Press rev. date: 03/23/2023

CONTENTS

ACKNOWLEDGMENTS

Thank you Justin, Kevin, and Henna. Questions from your perspective was golden.

Thank you to my mom, Diane, for all your feedback throughout this process. You're always there when I need you.

Thank you Melanie. As you know, it's all about the cover.

Thank you to my Spirit Guides for your very clear down loads of information. I am honored to have been a part of this creation. Thank you for choosing me!

Thank you to my husband, Keith, for cooking dinner when I was on a roll!

Thank you to my little doggie, Fancy, for all your patience as you watched me type with your ball in your mouth.

PREFACE

The Book You Wish You Were Born With

This book was written with all age groups in mind. Anyone from eighteen to 108 will benefit. While it is written in an easy-to-understand format with many descriptive and helpful analogies, the content is deep. This is the information we all need to have access to. As our society continues to go through a tremendous spiritual awakening, it is important to be aware of who we are beyond our physical nature. Whether you're retired and finally have time to contemplate the bigger picture, or you're young and just starting your life, this book can help free you of fears, limiting beliefs, and emotional pain. It can help bring a calm sense of clarity. Now, more than ever, we need to know how to have peace, joy, and love in our lives while understanding who we are spiritually.

When you start to grasp who you are beyond your physical body, you will start to recall how powerful you are! When you fully know you are not just a body but an energy being with goals, life begins to reshape from that uncomfortable place in which you find yourself to many expressions of Love Energy.

We all fall into heavy or low moments. Knowing how to find your way out and knowing how to create the life you want is what separates those who are joyful from those who live a life of mediocrity or misery.

Through understanding your Soul, you are able to understand there is no end to a person. No finality to a dimension. We can expand our awareness and realize there is so much more than what initially meets the eye. It's true that what cannot be seen can sometimes seem scary because it's unknown. But with knowledge, we can shed light on daunting thoughts and be liberated from the fears that stop us from reaching our full potential. This book will help you figure out how to replace low-vibrating energy with Love Energy. It will reassure you that you're not alone in this journey called life. It will show you how to leave painful moments in the past and take hold of the happiness you long for.

Start reading at the beginning or, you can start with the the glossary which is at the end of the book. The glossary will help you become familiarized with concepts that may be new to you. As you get further into the book you will find "Think About This" sections to help guide your thoughts more deeply on some subjects. If you're not in the mood for self-reflection, just skip over them or save them for another day. From there, let the information gently awaken your entire being. The content in this book is presented in a straightforward, easy-to understand style. Allow yourself to interpret the information the way it most naturally resonates with you. There is no right or wrong here, only what makes the most sense to you. Let go of needing to "stay inside the lines" and begin to listen to your inner voice. It may be quiet at first, but with practice and patience you'll be amazed at the clarity that follows. It's all here. Everything you need to find the happiness you were meant to have. Enjoy!

INTRODUCTION

Of course you're not your car! What a ridiculous statement! It's a catchy title though, isn't it? Did you see the title and say to yourself, *Wait, what? You're not your car? What does that even mean?* The next thing you knew you were right here reading these words. Don't worry. As you read the next couple of chapters the title of this book will become very clear. Trust me.

But first, how did this book find its way to you? Were you scrolling through search engines on your computer? Did a copy at the bookstore catch your eye? Was it a gift? Sure, any one of these possibilities could be what led you to the words you're reading right now, but it does go deeper than that. You found this book, and it found you, because of that *feeling* you have. You're starting to become more attuned to that *feeling* because it's making you aware there is something more extraordinary about your existence than what you were led to believe. You may not fully understand that *feeling* yet, but you're sure there's something bigger and better than what is plainly in front of you. You're awakening to a part of yourself that's absolutely amazing! Just as amazing as the powerful, unseen energy that led you to this book.

Ever since you were a child, you've been taught how to identify with yourself and your surroundings from the viewpoint of physicality. The obvious, tangible, conventional idea of you and your environment are what parents and teachers have led you to focus on. And they did this through no fault of their own! They are not to blame, because they, too, have only been taught the obvious, tangible, conventional part of themselves. How can teachers lead us to new ideas and places when new ideas and places are not in their awareness?

But now, the energy is changing on our planet. As it shifts, that *feeling* within you becomes stronger. That *feeling* is trying to get your attention, flag you down, and make you sit up and realize there are parts of you that have been out of your awareness for too long. It's trying to make you remember there is a *powerful place* within you that you need to find and if you let yourself follow that *feeling*, you will find it! You are realizing you need to learn who you are beyond your body. If you can know yourself as something more than just a physical body, your potential is limitless! Tapping into more of yourself can help you ride through the tough moments with ease, and it can help bring you to a place of joy and peace. If you can know yourself as something more than just a physical body, you will start to feel your own creative power, a power that brings success in all you do! A quiet part of you inherently knows this already. These ideas resonate with you. Deep within you it feels right, but it's just slightly out of reach. This is where that *feeling* is generated from. But how do you get there? How do you find that part of yourself?

What if joy and peace were yours to be had just by tweaking your thoughts? What if everything you ever attempted to do would end in complete success? Imagine it! Your own inner world full of bliss in which you experience a consent state of euphoric creativity! Colors are electrifying! Sounds are comforting, and smells are delicious! You move through your life with ease. It feels so good to be in such a loving state all the time! Thinking in this way is already making you feel like you're flying high, isn't it? Wow! What a fabulous world to live in, where everything is joy, peace, and success! Beauty everywhere and endless good feelings! A life like this is amazing! So many experiences to have at every corner. Can you feel it? C'mon, let's do this thing!

And then, *bam*! Like a stinging slap in the face, random people in your life do very uncool things that quickly wipe away this feeling of hope and euphoria. Or the media spells out the reality of what's really going on in the world, replacing your high, good feelings with despair, depression, and hopelessness. It's the truth! There are too many traumatic events happening on the planet right now, events that can make your attempt at peace and personal power seem out of reach and pointless. There are many traumatic things happening in the center of your very own life as well! But that *feeling* you have brings back your hope and an overwhelming knowing that the way of this world will change when more of us connect to that powerful part of ourselves. We must connect to it! As more and more people tap into that *feeling* they have, a new way of being will emerge. The trajectory of our planet and Universe is ultimately aimed toward great change, with peace and harmony at its core. To be a part of that change, it's imperative to first find the greater part of yourself. The true essence of who you are. You're not just a body! So stop acting like one.

What about serendipity? Serendipitous moments are like little flashlights that light up a path that's hard to see. They are bits of validation that we need to stay on that path, and they feel like bubbles of love that let us know we're not alone. Some people call them "God winks" or "the Universe at work," which basically means an event or moment so profound it seems to be orchestrated by higher intervention. Kismet is another great word. It means something that wasn't planned to happen but for unknown reasons did happen, thereby allowing some kind of good fortune into one's life. It doesn't really matter what you call it. What matters is recognizing when these things happen and understanding who you are through it all. Serendipitous moments should be aha moments (like finding this book), and in that moment you are once again reminded of that *feeling* that lets you know a wave of change is happening to the world. Great change doesn't happen all at once, and it can sometimes get a little messy. But with the right guidance, we can ride that wave with grace!

Whether you find yourself in serendipitous moments or stinging slap-in-the-face moments, it is so important to be aware of all parts of yourself and to understand the true essence of who you are. Both types of moments are the jumping-off place for something better to happen. You're not just the body you've been decorating all these years. You are a great force of beautiful energy that can create change for yourself, the world, and the Universe.

When you can feel, know, and experience yourself beyond your body, you will experience fundamental changes.

- You will feel the roadblocks in your life become much easier to get around, or they disappear entirely!
- You will notice relationships improving, or at the very least you will release feelings of hate.
- You will feel that those who have passed don't seem so far away.
- You will realize that creating better health inside your body can be as easy as following a formula.

These days it seems like children and teenagers are suffering more than ever before. Adults are struggling as well. Is it because of technology, overpopulation, our unclean food sources, greed, lack of morals and values, or an unclear vision of who we are? Whatever the culprit is that makes navigating life so difficult, you need to know you have the power to override these suffocating forces. But you've got to know who you are in order to know how to tap into your power. This book is about learning who you are beyond your physical body and understanding the power you have to create. It's really that simple! But first you must realize you're not only your body.

So who or what are we then?
A Soul ... A Body ... Chakras ...
That's who we are!

So why is this book entitled *You're Not Your Car*? You're about to find out in just a couple of more paragraphs, but first let's get clear on a couple things.

The word *Soul* has connections to religion as well as to spirituality. The content of this book, however, has no connection to religion whatsoever. It does not aim to approach concepts from a religious perspective. This book will examine ideas from the viewpoint of spirituality, which recognizes all individuals' prerogative to process information in a way that best resonates with their current state of evolvement. This book will cover concepts like limiting beliefs, karma, Soul's purpose, death, case studies, the UEF, why being different is so great, and other really interesting topics. How our feelings and Chakras ultimately affect our health will also be covered in some depth, including a "Deconstructed Chakra" section. You've already been told about the Glossary at the end of this book that defines words and concepts you may not be very familiar with. It's probably a good idea to go to the Glossary whenever you need to familiarize yourself with these words. In fact, I *highly recommend* you take a few minutes to look it over now. It will make reading this book much more enjoyable.

Please understand that it's impossible to simultaneously explain all the interconnected topics presented here. To fully understand each part, you must understand the other parts. As you read through the book and something doesn't make complete sense, be patient. Whatever is not clear will soon be answered as you get further along into the book. You will have moments of clarity as you turn each page. There is so much to know, so take your time and let each new concept marinate within your being. Now, let's get going and start with the most important part. You!

ONE

THE SOUL, THE CAR, A TANK, AND YOUR GANG

Who Are You? Who Who!

All of us are Souls who, for a variety of reasons, decided to incarnate into human form. To incarnate simply means to get into a vehicle that enables you the freedom to have experiences that are different from if you had stayed in your original form, which is pure energy. The vehicle we use is the human body!

The greatest, most delightful analogy I like to use to explain this concept is the idea of getting into your car. (But remember, you're not your car.) When you are in your car, driving down a busy highway, you are protected and able to maneuver among the other clunky cars. You may not be able to make your car dance, jump, spin, or skip like your body can, but it can definitely move you to where you want to go. You decide where you want to go, and your car takes you on the journey, allowing you to experience all the wondrous things along the way. Occasionally your outing takes unexpected turns and unexpected events happen. Sometimes the craziest of all crazy happens, and you find yourself having to make quick decisions, resulting in something good or ... not so good. As you pass by other cars you tend to see them as just the Honda, Mercedes, VW, or Ford, and not as actual people with a destination, or an intricate life, or a story that led them to who and where they are now. You do not connect with the people inside the car, so you don't know their story. You're unaware of their experiences, and you have no knowledge of how wonderfully special the driver of each car is. But if you did, you might learn they're just like you, heading for a destination but more importantly, experiencing along the way! If we all saw each other as people with destinations and reasons for those destinations, might we be a little more patient out there on the highway with each other? If we saw not just poor driving skills in a Honda, but a person who just endured a heartbreaking experience, would there be quite as much road rage? Can we see not just a Volkswagen, but a person who is late for his job because his child needed a little bit extra love and attention on this particular morning? And yes, he gave his child that love, but now he's late and being late again will have a terribly negative impact on his day, maybe his career. So he maneuvers quickly through traffic, upsetting every other driver along the way. But you don't know his life. You only know the Volkswagon, and you are thoroughly irritated with him. This is exactly what it's like to incarnate into the human body. Well, maybe not exactly like it, but goodness gracious it's a great analogy! Do you understand you are not your car? If you do, then can you understand you're not your body? You *are* your Soul! And, like driving a car, we are cruising through life in a body with a very specific journey in mind. If we can recognize the journey our fellow Souls are on, a journey with bumps, unexpected turns, and GPS devices that lose their signal from time to time, maybe we can cut them some slack and let up on *life* rage. We don't know each other's stories. We don't know why other Souls wanted another crack at this thing called physical living, yet here we all are, trying to live our best lives. We have intentions that we originally set out to experience before we got into these bodies, and the crazy, fun thing is every single one of us is having our own personalized experience, customized for ourselves by ourselves and actualized by way of the body.

So, who are you?

You are a Soul in a body who set out on a journey to know yourself from a physical perspective and to have many experiences. There are so many different types of experiences a Soul may want to gain insight on or evolve from, and I will give this concept more attention later. For now, let's continue painting the picture of the

Soul, because to understand your journey, you must first understand yourself.

Your Soul is the *true essence of who you are*. When you can grasp this construct in its entirety, you will read the word Soul and identify with it in the same way you identify with the words "you," "me," or "I." The true essence of who you are means the part of you that is indispensable. Without it, your body would not be what it is, nor would your mind possess the character that it does. Your essence is more important and more real than any other part of you. In its absence, there would be nothing else of you.

Take It Off! Take It Off!

As a fetus grows in utero, the Soul does not stay fixed within the body. Instead, it makes many visits in and out of the body as it starts to get used to its dense, slow-vibrating new environment. That is not to say the Soul isn't present during these months of fetus growth. It's just not constant over the nine-month period. The Soul doesn't need to be submerged inside the body to interact with the parents, its body, and the scenario it will be born into. The Soul is very much involved with its human existence from the start of conception (and even before) but does not need to be anchored into the body to be involved.

If you're trying to fully grasp the difference between the creative freedom felt as pure Soul energy, and the more confining feeling it experiences while getting used to existing in physical form, this next little analogy might help.

Remember the last time you had to dress up for a formal event? If you're a man maybe you wore a three-piece suit (on a hot and steamy summer day, no less!), T-shirt, dress shirt, tie, binding underwear, socks that cut off your circulation, and heavy, uncomfortable shoes (all of which were just a little bit tight because you gained a pound or two since the last time you had to wear your fancy gear). Ladies, you probably put on pantyhose, a pinching bra, Spanx, a slip, a short dress that you couldn't really bend over in if you didn't want to hear some stitches pop, and shoes that made you walk on your tiptoes like no creature on earth should ever be made to do. You could only sit with your legs crossed, and because it was the dead of winter your short skirt caused you to shiver all day. When it was all over, you raced home to your closet, stripped off all the torture garments, and replaced your confining clothes with baggy shorts and an oversized T-shirt (maybe not even any underwear!). And then you said, "Ah! That's better. I'm never wearing those ridiculous clothes again!" (Until the next time you got dressed up for a special occasion, of course.) The Soul feels like this when it's getting into its new body after uninhibited freedom as pure energy. That's why little visits in the beginning are a nice segue to spending the next one hundred years, plus or minus, in a body.

The Good Place or a Tank?

Where did your Soul (you) exist before you were born into a human body?

The realm that we use as our platform to have a human experience is what we also call earth or the physical world. So where and what is the "place" that we hang out in when we are not having a human experience on earth? It is the realm of Spirit created by Source. The easy name that most people are familiar with is heaven, so for our purposes here let's keep calling it heaven. But what is this place that we call heaven? Let's start with what it is not. It's not a destination. It's not *The Good Place* with Ted Danson and Kristen Bell. It does not follow the laws of physics, which require density and matter. It is not some place far off that we have no contact with while we are living out our human existence.

Are you with me so far?

The biggest thing that describes it is beautiful Love Energy from Source. (See the Glossary for the definition of Source.)

Side note: When we refer to Love and Love Energy in the context of spirituality, we are not referring to the hot and steamy romantic love between two lovers. It's also not the love you have for chocolate. It is the origin of all that is positive, brilliant, and wonderful. There are varying degrees of Love Energy and many different ways to express it. Different degrees would be joy, peace, kindness, compassion, tolerance, patience, and many, many more. Expressions of Love Energy are what we can see in everyday life, including acts of kindness between people, romantic love, moments of gratitude, happiness, patience, and so on. Love Energy is an endless form of energy from which everything that is good comes from. Imagine for a moment the vastness of the Universe and all that it contains. Much of the Universe is unknown and unseen, but within it there exists an endless well of Love Energy. Raw ingredients for all that is good comes from this genesis of Love Energy. Expressions of Love Energy can be seen in everyday life as a beautiful painting, a feeling you have for someone, acts of kindness, a peaceful carefree day, gratitude, a flower, compassion, self-worth, a hug, beautiful music, and on and on.

Now that you are clear on what Love Energy is, let's get back to the characteristics of heaven.

It is composed of beautiful Love Energy from Source. It is important to realize the "heaven" space is consistently all around us while we are here on the earth platform. We are in it now, and this energy flows organically and seamlessly among all that we sense. It is a beautiful energy that is forever flowing through and around everything we see and don't see. It contains vibrations of peace, joy, tranquility, creativity, euphoria, excitement, serenity, jubilation, love, enjoyment, passion, compassion, bliss, amazement, and so much more! (These are all subcategories of Love Energy.) The heaven space would be obvious to us if not for a metaphorical *veil* that keeps it concealed while we are in human form. And that seems so unfair to have this place of ultimate peace and love so close, only to be hidden away by our own lack of awareness! It is not because we are undeserving of such greatness. Instead, we chose to not be aware of it when we plopped into a body. To be fully exposed to such high-vibrating energy while we spend time in physical bodies that are somewhat limited by comparison would be a huge distraction. It would make the journey on earth even more confusing. But as you grow spiritually, the veil becomes thinner. Its importance starts to diminish as you allow yourself to become aware of and accepting of all that exists beyond physicality. Here's another great analogy to help you really grasp this. (You're going to start to see how much I love analogies as you go through this book!)

Imagine yourself in a very large tank. You have been in this tank for as long as you can remember, performing specific and important tasks. Everything you will ever need or want to sustain you or make your time enjoyable is there for you in the tank, except for windows (or so you think). The fact that there are no windows doesn't even come into your awareness because you have no baseline for this concept. The tank is floating in a breathtaking undersea world full of fascinating creatures, ultra-vivid colors, and enrapturing velvet sounds of peace and harmony. Everything about it is euphoric. These creatures happily exist in an extraordinary environment infused with bright warm light. They are well aware of you, because they can see in through the windows that you are not aware of. Keep in mind you would be able to see out to this alluring world if you chose to think in terms of the possibility of windows. If you allowed the concept of windows into your awareness, you would stop seeing your own reflection in the glass, and your eyes would refocus to perceive something more than you. Your eyes would shift from your reflection seen on the interior of the glass to the fantastic reality beyond the glass. Unfortunately, your focus stays limited. You only see yourself, and you have no idea you're floating in this beautiful underwater world. Inside your floating tank, there are clues everywhere that let you know the reality of your tank and the amazing environment outside that supports it. There are even books within your reach that explain the concept of windows and where you might find them in your surroundings. But you choose not to look at these clues. Instead, you prefer to think of yourself as alone, self-contained, and self-sufficient. Your thoughts of isolation are acceptable to both you and the creatures outside of your tank because you have free will, and all parties agree free will is of utmost importance. Regardless of your free will, shortsightedness, and self-sufficient feelings, the environment outside your tank continues to support your existence in all ways. It bears no ill will toward you or the fact that you're clueless. Actually, it's better you don't know what's beyond the tank, because the surreal peace and beauty out there would be very distracting. It could even make it hard for you to concentrate on and make sense of your life inside the tank. Maybe you would abandon your tank entirely to be a part of such glorious perfection.

No, you are not distracted. You are firmly grounded in your immediate surroundings, and you continue on with your tasks undisturbed and unenlightened in a windowless tank. This is similar to how we exist on earth with a "veil" gently obscuring reality from view. This analogy provides an understanding of how we Souls are in a body on earth and the energy of what we are calling heaven (and Source Energy) flows around us. The difference between the tank/undersea world and earth/heaven is that unlike the physical barrier that exists from the walls of the tank, there is no barrier between us and heaven and Source Energy. There is no separateness. There is only the veil that makes us completely unaware of the energy that weaves itself in, through, and around all aspects of physical existence. The only true barrier is our lack of awareness. As pure Souls, we know we will return to this beautiful space (in any capacity and configuration we wish). For some humans, the veil is starting to fray and thin. We are becoming aware of the concept of windows, so to speak. We are evolving with the incumbent shift that is already happening! We are allowing ourselves to be aware of both the tank as well as the *extraordinary environment infused with bright warm light*. Awareness is the most important ingredient for change.

As Souls, we know how valuable the human experience is and for this reason, we willingly and eagerly participate in earthly existences, again and again, knowing the veil exists to cloud our awareness. But the veil is definitely dissolving for many of us.

As we have already covered, the space beyond physicality is quite amazing. But the space within physicality is equally amazing, filled with experiences and moments not available to those existing in only energy form. I had the chance to sample one of these experiences in its most simplistic form. We all have these experiences, the difference here is I noticed it and will now cherish it.

I sat outside one fall afternoon with my husband (who is, by his own admission, not a deep and spiritual guy). The day was perfect. Cerulean blue sky, leaves on the brink of changing colors, sunlight covering our skin, temperature of the air warmed to perfection. But the most delicious part of this moment in time was the breeze blowing with just the right amount of force. My husband remarked how good the breeze felt. And then he said, "I'm going to miss how the wind feels on my skin when I'm dead." Somewhat shocked by his deep thought (because he actually had one), I immediately let my awareness go to my skin and the wind moving over it like a gentle feather. He was so right! I will miss it too. Little things like this will probably not be experienced without our bodies. So don't let those moments go by unnoticed. Thanks to him, I had a moment that I may have missed.

Your Gang Has iPhones

Though this book is not necessarily about Angels, Spirit Guides, and other energy that exists in Spirit, we still need to talk about them a little bit. Because in order to really grasp who you are, you need to know who your best friends are!

Before incarnating into your human body, you existed in the realm of Spirit as pure Soul energy. There are so many expansive things you can do in this realm but being in human form and interacting with physicality is not one of them. If you are currently here in human form, chances are you have chosen to have a human experience again for a very good purpose.

Before incarnating, you take inventory of all your experiences thus far from your previous lifetimes, time spent in Spirit, and anywhere else experiences can be had. You think long and hard about the experiences that still remain on your to-do list, so to speak. From there, you (as a Soul) have a pretty good idea of what you want your next life to be like in order to actually live out and feel these experiences. Next, you set up a "meeting" in the realm of Spirit with your Spirit Guides, Guardian Angel, and other Angels who offer help with your specific life plan. (See the Glossary for a clearer understanding of Guides and Angels.) There could have been other energy entities at this meeting as well. The point is this group comes together on your behalf and works together to set the wheels in motion for your incredible time spent on earth. But that isn't the end of this group. They are now your tribe, your posse, your entourage, your gang! They haven't left you. They have a vested interest in you. The love they have for you is extraordinary and continuous. It is so, so important to understand this! Quite often throughout our lives we find ourselves in moments where we feel utterly alone. We feel like no one understands us, and it is so painful to go on in this lonely place, feeling misunderstood and sad. If you do now or have ever felt like this, *stop right there!* You are not alone. Your gang is still with you, and the more you start to understand who you really are, the more apparent it will be that they are right there next to you, loving you. They never left you. They hold you, encourage you, support you, guide you in your most desperate moments. They rejoice with you in your best moments. They're holding out their energetic hands, waiting to give you a well-deserved high five. They are in your company through good times and bad. But it is so hard to feel them if you're not aware of all that you are beyond your physical body.

So you have a gang, a plan, a Soul, a body, and you are completely unaware of all of it (except for your body). As you move through your human life, you can become derailed from your original plan, and that's where your Guides will try to give you a nudge back on track. (These nudges are examples of serendipitous moments or God winks.) They may even give you a big ole push, but you have free will that supersedes all. So they push, you ignore, and off the course you will go. Or they push, you get back on course, and everyone takes a big sigh of relief.

As for your Guardian Angel, this is a being that loves you unconditionally. Unconditionally! Are you getting that? Unconditionally! Like you love your little doggie unconditionally, even when he tinkles on the carpet. You might get mad for a minute, but then you're back to smooches for little Rexi the puppy. Your Guardian Angel loves you even more than that. If you tinkled on the carpet, your Guardian Angel wouldn't get mad for a minute, not even a second. Your Guardian Angel is your biggest fan, number one supporter, and never, ever leaves your side. Angels are androgynous, meaning they are sexless, but your Guardian Angel can take on the qualities of male or female depending on your needs. For example, if you are a woman and a female Guardian Angel would make it easier for you to feel like you and your Angel are your besties, then female energy is what you will feel from "her." Or imagine you are a soldier in battle. A very strong, dominant force of male energy may make you feel safer. These two examples are only examples. This is not to say that only a woman can be a bestie for a woman or only a man can have strong warrior energy. An Angel's qualities will reflect the needs of the human. Mix and match! You get the picture. Guardian Angels stay in their angel form for the most part. This means most people won't be able to see them (unless they are clairvoyant).

Side Note: The next section touches on the topic of vibrational frequency, which will be covered in depth later in this book. Since there is reference to it now, here is a brief description. High and low vibrating frequency can be found in the Glossary.

Everything in the Universe is energy and everything in the Universe vibrates. Our own bodies vibrate at a specific frequency and each part of our bodies vibrate with their own vibrational frequencies. When you raise your own vibrational frequency, the energy at your disposal is more powerful and your ability to create is amplified. There are ways to raise your vibrational frequency, some of which you probably do on a regular basis and don't even realize it.

The vibrational frequency of an Angel is very high, and our human eyes do not have the sensitivity to see frequencies that vibrate at such a high rate. But once you become more aware of yourself beyond your physical body, you will begin to sense things that exist beyond your physical boundaries. Your Guardian Angel is one of those things you will sense (and maybe even see as you develop your clairvoyance). Having said this, you should also know that there are times when Angels will manifest into physical form. If it is of the utmost importance that a message, help, or nudge get to you, Angels and even Spirit Guides can slow their vibration enough to be seen, heard, or known with human senses. They may present themselves as just a random person you have a brief encounter with, or someone who becomes your friend. Rarely, if ever, will they be people who are permanent fixtures in your life. The permanent people are other Souls who have their own plans that somehow coincide with yours. Our gang can also cause synchronicities to happen, create situations that provide you with a message (like a song on the radio), or a myriad of other fascinating phenomenon to get your attention. When Angels and Spirit Guides slow down their vibrational frequency to communicate with us, it requires immense energy on their part and would be what we consider exhausting to do. A much more effective and collaborative way to communicate is to meet each other halfway.

Consider this:

You are aware there are such things as Angels, but you have no concept of who *you* are beyond your physical body. You're wondering why you are not getting messages from Angels. That would be similar to your Angel calling you on your iPhone, but you're picking up your old-fashioned house phone to see if there's an Angel there. There is absolutely no connection.

Next, consider this:

You are aware of Angels. You are aware you are a Soul existing on an earth platform surrounded by Love Energy. You know your Guardian Angel is with you and loves you, and this idea feels very good to you. In moments of crisis, you want to feel support from your Guardian Angel, but your vibrational frequency as a human is much slower than the vibrational frequency of Angels. You are open and willing to hear from your Guardian Angel, but nothing seems to be coming through. This is as if you were both using iPhones, but you haven't charged your battery in a while. You see you're getting a call, but when you go to answer the phone, it goes dead. You feel like you were so close to getting the message because you were actually aware the phone was ringing. Gosh! So close! You have thoughts of your mother saying, "Don't forget to charge your phone before you leave the house!" (That's what I'm always saying to *my* kids, anyway.)

And now consider this:

You are aware of Angels, and in fact you have a wonderful relationship with your Angels and Spirit Guides. In times of crisis *and* joyfulness, you are able to connect with your entire gang because you have learned how to *feel* them. You have learned that meditating, surrounding yourself with Love Energy, quieting your mind, and spending time in nature are ways to raise your vibrational frequency. Your vibrational frequency is high enough that it provides you with subtle communication with Angels, Spirit Guides, and Source Energy. This is like when you're on your cell phone and the connection is pretty good. You're communicating, but every now and then you find yourself saying "Can you hear me now? Can you hear me *now*? Oh, okay. Good. I can hear you too." But then you move to the other side of the room and you're back to "Can you hear me now? I can kinda hear you." Even though this isn't the best connection, you're still getting the gist of the conversation. This is great! You're communicating with your gang. It takes work. You're not going to have a perfect connection right away, or even all the time. Some amount of communication and feeling your gang around you often is exponentially better than feeling isolated, alone, scared, and sad.

If you want a very clear signal all the time, you have to stay at a very high vibrational frequency as much as you possibly can. It's so much easier to do than you may think, but it does take dedication as well as changing your outlook on life. Don't worry, we will talk a lot about raising your vibrational frequency a little bit later.

If your vibrational frequency is not high, you may never be aware of your Guardian Angel sending you Love Energy, and that's okay. You don't need to be aware for the energy to reach you. It's like when you've had a really bad day. Your energy is low, so you turn on the TV to be distracted, but you still feel like the inside of a garbage disposal. Unbeknownst to you, your little doggie is sitting on the floor, looking at you with big heart emoji in his eyes while you watch the TV. You may not be aware of his love, but it doesn't mean little Rexi isn't adoringly gazing at the number one dog owner in the world. It's not his fault you won't look over at him to see all that love. But nonetheless, he's still sending you tons of unconditional doggie love.

Right now, think back and try to remember your most dire moments. You needed love more than ever, but you felt very alone in the world. No one understood you. No one cared, and your heart ached. Can you think of a time you felt like this? You need to understand in the very moment you felt like that your Guardian Angel was loving you, unconditionally, and with intense energy.

At the very least, it would have been enough energy to calm your aching heart so you could hold your head above water long enough to let go of some of that pain and understand your situation with a little bit more clarity. So, like little Rexi, the love was there for you to have. The question is, were you aware it was there for you? It's so much harder to know the gang and all the love that is being offered to you if you are not fully aware of the true essence of who you are. You are Soul! And you are never alone.

Do you feel like you're starting to understand that part of yourself just a little bit more?

The Monkey Told Me to Do It

As we have already discussed, your Soul came with a plan, or at the very least knew what it wanted to experience. Your body and your mind probably don't have access to that plan. Remember, your body grew from one little cell and you (Soul) and your gang had that initial meeting some point before this (or possibly after depending on the circumstances). Your body is completely unaware of what the plan is. It's literally just your vehicle to get around in. There was, however, input from you (Soul) and your gang as to what style of body you would have to help fulfill the kind of experience(s) you wanted to have in this lifetime. Realize that no matter what you look like, you look perfect! You look exactly the way you (Soul) wanted to look to have the experience you thought would best serve you at this time. Remember there is a much bigger picture going on, but that veil is annoyingly in front of your eyes, keeping you from seeing that picture with complete clarity. When you start to know yourself as Soul, you will understand you are absolutely amazing, perfect, and beautiful just the way you are. Even if that means your intent is to completely change how you physically look. We will dive deeper into the subject of "you're beautiful just the way you are" after we lay down a few more foundational concepts.

Your mind is consciousness, a place from which you react to the outside world. It is also a place where energy from your Soul is converted into thoughts and then carried out in physical form. Think of your mind as the bridge between your Soul and your body. So, to outwardly know your Soul self, your mind needs to go within. It needs to connect with the Soul as it resides in the body. When you are able to connect with that part of you, remarkable changes will take place:

- You will be able to access the navigational system you came with.
- You will reconnect with that joy and peace you "floated" in before incarnating.
- You will begin to recall your intentions.
- You will understand how and where to find happiness.
- You will feel calm, serene, and joyful.
- You will find your answers and your inner knowing.

And all this can be had for the low, low price of learning to meditate! That's right. Meditating (along with a few other things) will bring you very close to your Soul and all it has to offer. Meditating has become more and more popular in recent years, which is a wonderful thing! Some people, however, are scared off or turned off by it. They think it seems complicated, or the monkey mind starts to get a little too active. The monkey mind likes to swing around from thought to thought. It hollers things at you—what you need to do, what you want to do, what you already did, what you should be doing, and just about anything else that is distracting.

Meditation can offer so many benefits, but like many other things, it's a practice. The first day you tried to walk, you most likely tumbled down, a lot. But with practice you got better and even learned to run! What else can you think of that you tried, failed, practiced, mastered, and now it's easy-peasy lemon squeezy?

One of the most useful reasons to meditate, which brings you in touch with your Soul and all its (your) wisdom, is the information coming from it (you) is real. If you don't listen to your Soul and only hear the chatter in your monkey mind or the untruths being told outside of you, you will succumb to a myriad of negative thoughts, none of which are a part of your Soul's plan. Remember, your Soul is the part of you that consists of Love Energy. It is the only main recurring component of each human being you were in all your past lives, so it holds enormous amounts of wisdom. In addition to the monkey, your mind also has within it something called the ego, unfortunately. The ego is mean, rarely comes from a place of love, and does not have access to wisdom. Have you ever heard these comments inside your head (whether they be background or foreground thoughts)?

You are not good enough.   You are not funny enough.

You are not smart enough.   You are not creative enough.

You are not thin enough.   You are not tall enough.

You are not pretty enough.   You are not sexy enough.

You are not strong enough.   You are not lovable enough.

You are not wealthy enough.   You are not _____.

These are *not* thoughts coming from your Soul. The ego is the part of your mind that is always ready to tell you you're less than you are, or that bad things are in store for you. If you hear anything other than positive, love-based statements or thoughts when you meditate, the monkey mind is in full swing and has let the ego out of its cage. The part of you that has the most complete and accurate information about who you are as a total being is your Soul. Do not listen to the monkey mind. Do not listen to the ego. Learn to meditate with ease. Learning and practicing is the key. Think about the first day of class when you were learning a foreign language. Did you go full on into conversation like it was your first language? No, you probably sounded a little ridiculous. The same goes for meditating. The thoughts that come through your mind are going to be a little ridiculous. Just as ridiculous as the negative thoughts your ego is pumping out at you all day. Don't let your initial meditations be the determining factor for how good you're going to be at it. Learn to tone down the monkeys and the ego. Allow your Soul to find its voice. Be patient, release judgment over yourself, and realize you need to exercise your meditation muscles just like you need to exercise your body muscles.

Just a Drop

The creation of your Soul came from the purest of origins. It (you) was spawned from Source Energy. This means you came from Source, and you are Source. Love Energy, as well as all that follows Love, vibrates within Source Energy and has the potential to create with infinite possibilities. Every single thing or thought in the Universe that has vibrational frequencies of positivity is an expression of Love Energy. We, as Souls, are expressions of that energy! We are the beautiful light that can give rise to perfection as we see it, and it is done through the power of our intentions and through our connection to Source Energy. We are all a part of Source Energy, and because of this, we are all connected to each other. As individual parts of Source Energy, we are wondrous, creative beings. As a connected and combined loving force of Source Energy, we can create beyond rational imagination!

Wow! That's a mouthful! So let's go ahead and break that down into something we can work with.

My favorite way to explain the Soul, Source Energy, and how we are all connected is to use the "drop of water from the sea" analogy. Sadly, I did not come up with this analogy myself. It's been around for eons. But I do believe I embellished it a bit!

When we stand in awe of the sea, we realize its amazing power, feel its tranquil beauty, acknowledge it as a giver of life, and we feel its endless limits as we catch sight of the horizon where there seems to be no boundaries. All who have experienced the sea are left feeling a calm wholeness.

But what if you take an eyedropper and suck up just one drop of that sea? In a standard dropper, that would be about one-twentieth of a milliliter. That is a tiny, tiny bit of sea! Then place that one little drop of sea in an empty cup. Is the sea in the cup? Or is that drop of water no longer the sea? Is it just a wet spot at the bottom of a cup? It still possesses all the chemical and biological components from that which it came from. Why would it be anything less than the sea?

Now make the parallel between the sea and Source Energy. Like the little drop of water, our Souls are a small part of Source Energy. Each one of us is a drop taken from the whole. After every Soul is born, the creative power from Source is intact and limitless! We can create, become, or feel anything we want because we are powerful creators from the inexplicably beautiful Source Energy.

Don't limit yourself! Know you are wonderful, beautiful, and powerful!

This analogy gets you thinking, doesn't it? But remember, the sea (Source) has spawned you. Has created you. It is your parent. And while there are many powerful components in the drop of water, there is much the drop must experience to transcend beyond its current perceived limitations. The magnitude of its wholeness is not yet understood by the drop of water.

When your Soul finishes with its human experience in this lifetime, it will exit the body, but who you are stays intact. The memories and experiences you've had are imprinted on your Soul and become part of your Soul's energy, whether it was from this lifetime or from any one of the many lifetimes before. There is no part of your human experience that is lost, forgotten, or changed after you depart from the physical realm. In fact, once you have shed the heavy, cumbersome, and sometimes distracting physical body, you perceive all events and interactions you have had in your physical existence with amazing perceptibility.

As you're starting to get to know who you really are, are you starting to understand just how amazing you are? Do you realize what a powerful, creative being you are? Do you recognize yet you're not just that body, just as we certainly are not our cars? If you're not feeling just how mind-blowingly remarkable you are yet, don't worry. We're still only on the first chapter.

Anchoring, Buzzing, and Walking Away

As we've said, your Soul is energy, and so it doesn't follow the rules of physicality. When we talk about the location of the Soul, it is very different from talking about the location of your brain, or liver, or heart.

Everything in the Universe vibrates. That is an indisputable fact of science. Our organs and our bodies have a vibrational frequency that is very slow compared to our Soul. They have to be slow in order for them to do the jobs they were designed to do on the physical plane. Our true essence (our Soul) is pure energy and therefore vibrates much faster. For that reason, you cannot dissect the body and find the Soul as you could the heart. It can't be seen by the human eye because it's vibrating too fast. It can't be detected by mechanical instruments. There is evidence that Kirlian Photography can capture the auric field or the energy around living things. But the Soul cannot be seen mechanically or electronically because it vibrates much to fast.

You can feel the Soul, though. It is certainly possible to feel your own Soul and even possible to feel someone else's Soul, living in physical and living out of physical. This means you can feel the presence of someone's Soul as they sit inside a body next to you, as well as feel a Soul that is free of a human body—otherwise known as a deceased person. It is your own Soul, in fact, that feels other Souls. It has this ability because of a heightened intuitive sense. When you are aware of your Soul and allow the energy of it to completely fill your physical body, your capabilities and senses are enhanced, including your intuitive sense.

These days we are all so focused on what we can see. And what it is that we see on the TV, on our iPhone, on our computer, on our social media, and in big cities is information being blasted out at us, much of which is useless information. Many of us have forgotten how to feel. In ancient times, feeling (which is different from *feelings* and different from touch) was just as important to a successful life as the other five senses. If you think your sense of feeling has gone dormant, there are so many fun ways to wake it up.

1. **Body Buzz**. Sit comfortably and quietly. Turn off all electronics around you. Turn your attention inward and start to feel your body. Feel the weight of your body connecting with the chair or floor. Notice if anything feels a little achy. Notice if your digestion is rumbly or quiet. Connect with the physical part of yourself. Without placing your hand on your chest, start to feel your heart beating in your chest. Spend some time really connecting with your heart and the movement it creates within you. Now redirect your attention to a more elusive place of your being. Go beyond your physical body, almost like your dropping down to a hidden part of yourself. In that space become aware of a very slight, vibrating feeling throughout all of you, though it is most discernible in your chest. It's very subtle. It won't be as obvious and loud as your heart beat. It's not a physical feeling. It is a slight and vaporous buzz. Sit with that small buzz, and slowly start to mute out the physical body feelings you initially felt. The longer you sit with that gentle vibration, the more

apparent it will become. This buzz you feel is your energy body, and it can be amplified through intention.

2. **Tree Hugger.** This is similar to the exercise above, except this time you will be feeling the energy of a tree. Go outside and find a healthy tree. Standing about ten feet away, just take some time to look at it. Look at the roots, trunk, bark, branches, leaves (color and shape), unusual markings, and seeds or fruit it bears. Take in that tree and see it for what it really is. Try to look at it in a way you have never looked at a tree before. Really let your eyes absorb every detail. Now walk up to the tree and put your arms around it. Let your whole body make contact with it. Let your attention be directed only to the tree and allow your awareness to find its way into the tree. Be still. Now you will start to feel the life of that tree. If you stay there long enough you may feel the buzz you felt in yourself, or it may induce an intoxicatingly peaceful emotion. This is the tree enswathing you into its energy (and its love). Generally speaking, the bigger the tree, the easier it is to be successful with this exercise. It will also be easier to do if you are in nature as opposed to being on the side of an interstate highway.

3. **Earth Energy.** This is very similar to the tree exercise. This time lay your body (face up or face down—try them both) on the earth, making complete contact. Close your eyes and imagine the dirt below you. Now imagine each layer of dirt and rock below that. It doesn't matter if you're not a geologist. Just let your imagination take you to the center of the earth. Feel the massiveness of the earth. Feel the strength of the earth. Feel the earth holding you, supporting you within the endless Universe. Let your brain and your mind become aware of the massive size of the earth compared to yourself. You will start to feel a gentle push against your own energy. This push is the support and strength of the earth's energy. Let yourself take a deep sigh of comfort knowing the earth is there for you, providing constant strength and support.

4. **Feel the Room.** Before you start this exercise, prepare yourself by doing the Body Buzz exercise. Then walk into a room that has at least two people in it. If they don't expect someone to enter the room, even better. Now try to feel the energy in the room. Does something feel very heavy, like heavy smog laying on your shoulders or head? Do you instantly get a worried feeling? Does the space and the air feel clean and light? Know that you are not noticing yourself in this exercise. You are noticing the energy in the room created by the people in it.

When you start to get very proficient at feeling energy, you will see you can use it in much more sophisticated ways. You will start to feel the energy of a loved one, which will help you to know how to approach them. You will feel the energy of a pet, which will help you to know how to interact them. You will feel the energy of a situation, which will give you information on how to proceed. With practice, you will even feel the energy of unseen things in a room or house. Ultimately, you can feel the energy of anything, which will give you one more piece of information to allow you to make decisions that will be in your highest and best interest. Feeling translates into knowing and it is a powerful sense to have. These exercises will also help you develop your claircognizance and clairsentience."

Well, that was yet another tangent! Let's get back to finding the Soul.

A widely accepted way to describe Soul location is to say it is anchored in the body at the center of the chest next to the heart. Having said that, if you are more comfortable envisioning the Soul in a different location, that is perfectly fine. It is not a fixed entity like the heart, which will never move out of its location (hopefully!). The Soul (you) is energy and has the power to inhabit all, part, or none of the body. But traditionally it is said that the Soul is firmly anchored in the body at the location next to the heart.

When we meditate and fully activate our Soul's power, the Soul should exist throughout the entire body, and even beyond the parameters of the body into the auric field. To do this, we use our intention. Intentions are thoughts. Thoughts are energy. Energy is powerful. So to move your Soul's presence throughout your entire body, just intend for this to happen. And so it does.

To get the most complete picture of what we are, I will just briefly explain the auric field here. Your auric field is energy, and it exists all around you, starting from your physical body and expanding out about three feet from there, although you can manipulate the size of it through meditation and intention. Anything living has this type of field, including humans, animals, insects, plants, trees, and the planet. Each of these living things has a slightly modified field compared to humans. Even though non-human auric fields are different, they still operate with perfection, serving each living entity as needed. Our human auric field has seven layers, which are the physical, etheric, emotional, mental, spiritual, cosmic, and nirvanic fields. The energy from your Chakras is not only present in your auric field. It also creates your auric field and is the determining factor for size, color variations, and clarity of your auric field. Because your Chakras reflect your overall health, your auric field will change shape and color based on your mood, physical health, mental stability, spiritual awareness, and emotional changes. Children are very adept at seeing the auric field of others, but eventually they are taught logic and limiting beliefs. As they identify more and more with "societal norms", children will become firmly rooted in physicality. When this happens, the natural ability to see auric fields fades away. If you are with a child who happily reports seeing beautiful blobs of color around people, enthusiastically encourage them to talk in detail about what they are seeing. Not only will this help them to feel confident in who they are, it will also help nurture their psychic abilities and spiritual connection.

The etheric layer of our auric field is a blueprint of our physical body. Regardless of the injury or disease that may effect the physical body, the blueprint remains unblemished. Through intense meditation we can heal our physical body via the etheric body.

It is a matter of merging the flawless energy in the etheric layer with the physical body that is sick or injured. This does, however, require many hours of dedicated meditation, positive thinking and nurturing the physical body. It's not something that can be done on a whim and without intense focus.

Using your intention, you can make your Soul (and your auric field) as big as you want. As you use your thoughts to intend for your Soul to swell past the body, it will happen. Remember, your thoughts are very powerful.

So let's keep going deeper into understanding the Soul. To do so let's visit the "You're Not Your Car" analogy again, but differently. (You know you love this analogy too!) Your body is very much like a vehicle. Think about your car. It's pretty on the outside when it's new (so is your body). If you take care of it, it will stay looking new for a while (like your body) but with time the car will get scratched and need some of its parts repaired (and your body might need a couple of parts repaired too). When you get inside of it, you know you're safe from things like the pouring rain, cold temperatures, crazy drivers, bugs splatting onto your face, and other hazards of the physical world while en route to your destination. (and inside your body, your Soul knows it is in a perfect place to have experiences).

Your little car takes you everywhere! And together you have so many wonderful adventures and experiences (just like you do when you're inside your body). But there will come a day when your car gets old enough that you just can't make it go another mile. At that time, you will probably get out of it and have a quiet moment with your car, just the two of you and maybe the mechanic too. Then you'll walk away, looking forward to your next car and new adventures.

The similarities are amazing! And just like your car, your body is temporary. But while you are in it, the body provides a way for the energy part of you (Soul) to move about on earth. Your body lets you hear, smell, taste, see, feel and interact with others from a very different perspective than it would be able to do if it were limited to energy form. Limited, that is, on a physical plane. But in Spirit, the Soul is a boundless powerful creative force. It is this creative force that we *can* and *should* tap into while residing in the body.

Free Will

Like a car, you have a course set on the GPS, but you also have free will. Free will lets you take side roads or change the destination all together. You may find a path to go down other than what was originally intended. And that's not a problem, as long as it stays somewhat in line with what your Soul wanted to seek out and experience in this lifetime. If your path goes too far astray from what your original intent was, there are very active participants in your "gang" who have been chosen and are dedicated to helping you stay on your path. This gang is the spiritual group you came here to this earth with. As mentioned before, it can consist of Angels, Spirit Guides, and possibly ascended masters. But even with these helpers trying to keep you on your Soul path, free will is always the deciding factor. As an incarnated human being, you can always exercise free will, and the entire plan you originally decided on goes out the window. So long as your free will actions don't hurt anyone else, there's absolutely nothing wrong with straying from the intended path, except you may not be able to participate in the experiences you as a Soul initially set out to have.

Think About This

Have you ever thought of yourself as something more than the human body that you inhabit? Take a moment now to consider yourself as a Soul inside your body.

- Close your eyes and bring your attention to the center of your chest.

- Take some slow deep breaths.
- Inhale four counts.
- Exhale five counts.
- Do this deep breathing for about a minute.
- Think about the powerful energy that is your Soul shining brightly in your chest.
- What color is it? What shape? How big?
- Use your mind's eye to envision as many details about your Soul as you can.
- Now start to transition your thoughts to these concepts:
- Your Soul is the true essence of who you are, and your body is temporary.
- Your Soul knows all the important, everlasting parts of who you are, and your body is the container.
- Your Soul and body are bridged together by the mind. Your Soul is the control center, but your mind is the two-way radio that brings thoughts into the body and brings sensations and experiences from the body to the Soul.
- You *are* your Soul forever.
- Your body is beautiful yet temporary.
- Stay here in this mini meditation for as long as you like while you integrate these revelations. When you are through, record your thoughts in a journal.

For longer, fuller guided meditations, go to
www.mindfulbodywithsoul.com/meditations
Here you will find recorded guided meditations for Chakra Balancing, relaxing and raising your vibration, and harnessing your powerful creative energy.

TWO

GETTING COMFORTABLE WITH CHAKRAS

What If You Didn't Know

So far, we know we are Souls, which are a part of Source Energy. We also know our bodies are the vehicles we use to move about the physical realm. And we have a basic understanding of our energy field. In addition to these parts, we also have a Chakra system.

If you're new to the topic of Chakras, don't worry. It can be overwhelming to learn about this brand-new concept, but like everything else in this book, I will first present the full concept and then break it down. By the end of this section, you will have a fabulous understanding of Chakras.

Let's start with what most of us already understand: the physical body you use to cruise around the planet. Though you may not fully understand all its inner workings like a medical professional or scientist, you do know you have these systems:

- Cardiovascular
- Digestive
- Endocrine (Hormones)
- Integumentary (Skin)
- Lymphatic
- Muscular
- Nervous
- Reproductive
- Respiratory
- Skeletal
- Urinary

These systems all work together, and when they are working the way they should, you experience good health. If any one of these systems becomes out of balance, you may feel the effects of it throughout your body. For example, if you have cancer, you may also experience fatigue, weight loss, temperature fluctuations, pain. We depend on all parts to work correctly and when they don't, we feel very not okay. You may even find that other systems begin to work improperly.

Now, what if you did not know one of your systems existed? What if you had a stomach ache but you had absolutely no knowledge of a digestive system within your body? Would you think your heart fell into your belly? Would you be worried a bone broke and was poking into your abdominal muscles?

Luckily, this is not something you have to stress out about because you are well aware of the digestive system and one way or another, you will get that stomach ache figured out.

Well, there's another system fixed in our entire being that interacts with the physical body. It is the Chakra system, and it's very important to have at least a basic understanding of what it's all about. Navigating through life and maintaining health in the physical body becomes so much easier when you can answer these questions about the Chakra system:

- What is it?
- Where is it?
- What does it do?
- How do we know when it's not functioning right?
- What makes it become out of balance?
- What does imbalance feel like?
- How do we fix it?

It's true this system can seem a bit more mysterious because it can't be seen with the human eye like our other systems. Let's dispel that notion right away by comparing it to other unseen, yet real things. Our emotions are unseen, but there is no dispute they exist. Our ideas are unseen, but we have them. Air, which is essential to life, cannot be seen with our naked eye, yet we know it is there and are quite aware when it is not.

Our Chakra system is a system of energy that cannot be seen, but it is an essential part of maintaining our human body.

It is designed to work as a forerunner that metabolizes (processes) incoming emotional encounters. The Chakras metabolize energy from these experiences so they can be felt in our current reality. If the experience is perceived as negative, the Chakra will metabolize it into the body as negative. When the Chakra has repetitive perceived experiences that are negative, it will most likely set it out of balance. If a Chakra metabolizes the energy of a major singular emotional experience that is perceived as negative, it will also set the Chakra out of balance. (It is important to understand what is a perceived negative experience. Negative energy comes from an experience that the individual perceives as not good, unwanted, harmful, distasteful, disastrous, unkind, non-beneficial, hateful, etc. When an expectation is not met, the experience is felt as negative. In reality, the experience is neutral. It is only our subjective interpretation of the thing or event that assigns a negative or positive energy to it. Please go to the Glossary to read the entire entry for Energy in order to be clear on what is a perceived negative experience.)

These first few paragraphs may feel a little overwhelming. But don't worry. I'm going to break it down for you and give you many analogies. It's what I do!

Here's an analogy of a repetitive negative experience that will hopefully make this section on Chakras a little clearer. The purpose of this analogy is to highlight the end result of a repetitive negative experience. Please keep in mind this is just an anecdotal example with no factual evidence regarding speed, material, or injury. Please do not attempt this example yourself.

You and your little car are out for a drive. You feel well equipped because your car has seat belts, antilock brakes, and airbags. You are driving along, and for some reason you decide to drive your car straight into a wall at thirty-five miles per hour. *Why* you decide to drive your car into a wall at this speed is imponderable to all yet, inconceivably, here you are doing it. Your airbag goes off, seat belt activates. Basically, you're unhurt, thanks to the airbag and seat belt. But then, the baffled crowd of gaping mouthed eyewitnesses watch you back up thirty yards, accelerate to thirty-five miles per hour again, and crash into that wall again. And again! And again! We do a speedy time lapse and hours later you're still at it, crashing your car into the wall. (In this example, let's assume your car's exterior is withstanding the smallest amount of damage because it is made from a composite of metal and graphene, the strongest material on earth.) But the safety mechanisms are wearing out. The seat belt is beginning to fray, and your used airbag is just a deflated pile of nylon and polyester in your lap. Finally, the last thread of your seat belt breaks, and your head hits the steering wheel, leaving you with a painful headache and a few stitches. It's obvious the body of your car has, by this time, taken quite a bit of abuse as well, despite its tough exterior. Like your Chakras, the seat belt interprets the energy of an event. It metabolizes the force and creates an impactful jarring feeling on your body each time it activates (think of these jarring feelings as emotions). The first one or two times you become aware of the jarring feeling should be enough for you to ascertain that something in this scenario is not right. The more you expose yourself to these emotions, the more your Chakra becomes out of balance and your body begins to suffer.

The energy of a perceived experience travels through the Chakra where the energy is processed. That energy eventually makes its way into the endocrine system, where hormones create an appropriate emotional response that you can feel on a human level. An example of a *repetitive emotional imbalance* would be if you were constantly told your opinion doesn't matter (which, in time, would cause an imbalance in a Chakra or Chakras, similar to the threads of a seatbelt wearing away). An example of a *major singular emotional experience* that happens once would be a violent rape in which the experience is processed as horrific, causing immediate imbalance to a Chakra or Chakras. Using the seat-belt reference, it would be equivalent to the seat belt immediately severing apart after an initial impact of one hundred miles per hour. Most probably but not definitely, rape would create imbalance in the Sacral Chakra. This Chakra metabolizes feelings like guilt, shame, pain, unworthiness, and victimization. In time, both these examples will create a physical disease. The imbalance in the Sacral Chakra could cause reproductive problems or uterine cancer for example. Just as the car exterior slowly breaks down, your body also breaks down.

If you started this chapter with little or no understanding about Chakras, hopefully you're beginning to get more clarity on this topic. If not, don't worry! There's so much more to know. Let's keep going.

Here's a quick recap: Chakras keep us functioning and connected to other people and our surroundings. They decipher the emotions we feel as we react to each experience we have. They absorb energy from all our interactions, and then that energy is metabolized into emotions and feelings.

The bullets below explain how energy moves through the Chakras and into our bodies. (Everything in the Universe is energy that vibrates. Even an emotional interaction between people is energy.)

- Energy from a situation comes in to one or more of the Chakras.
- The energy is a certain degree of positive or negative, depending on how it is perceived.
- That energy passes through the Chakra and into energy pathways in our body (also known as nadis).
- There are 72,000 nadis that spring from three main nadis.
- From the energy pathway, the information, still in the form of energy, is sent through the nervous system (NS).
- The NS brings the information to the endocrine system where it is made into hormones.
- Hormones are secreted into the blood and circulated to where they are needed (we are not just talking about sex hormones here, but every hormone in the body).
- Because hormones regulate every function of our physical body, we are dependent on them to keep every part of our body in top-notch health.

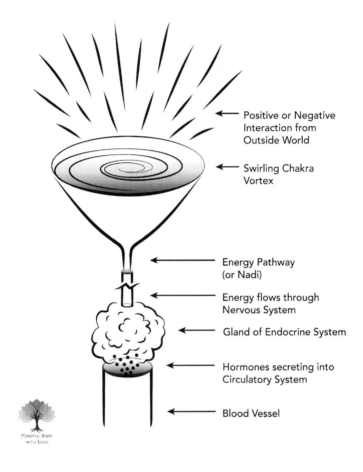

Positive or Negative
Interaction from
Outside World

Swirling Chakra
Vortex

Energy Pathway
(or Nadi)

Energy flows through
Nervous System

Gland of Endocrine System

Hormones secreting into
Circulatory System

Blood Vessel

The positive or negative interaction with the outside world is a perceived interpretation. If it is perceived as negative, that energy flow will eventually create hormones that produce an emotion to fit the perceived interpretation. If the emotion is negative, and that emotion stays with us indefinitely (or is repetitive), the body continues to be affected by it and eventually disease is established. The same happens from a positive perceived interpretation. This will have great benefits to the body.

This is important to understand so let's say it again a little differently.

Repetitive means an emotion that comes up again and again. When you have a repetitive, negative emotional event, it will negatively impact the energy flow within your Chakras. Your Chakras can equally be compromised by a major singular emotional event that you cannot let go of. When either of these happen, a Chakra will become imbalanced. The energy flow within your Chakras will not be able to support the parts of the physical body it governs, and over time, disease can develop.

One more time!

Your Chakras can be compromised in two ways.

A repetitive, emotional event that you perceive as negative occurs with some degree of frequency. In time your Chakras will become out of balance and eventually the body will suffer.

Or

A singular emotional event occurs that is unbearable and emotionally upsetting to you. If you are not able to let go of the emotional pain it causes, an imbalance in the Chakra system will manifest, eventually causing physical malfunctions.

In both these scenarios, as well as *all* difficult and emotional events in life, it is important to be able to leave the painful emotion in the past with the event that caused it. Experiencing and feeling the emotion to its fullest is good and necessary. When it is over, you must leave it in the past with the energy of the event. Of course, this is much easier said than done! Sometimes we humans need to find the courage and strength to let go of these emotions. Sometimes, we aren't ready to acknowledge them in order to let them go. Fear can still be holding on, almost paralyzing us from letting go. We may not be able to forgive either ourselves or the offender yet. Living with the emotional pain can sometimes be easier then working through it to leave it in the past. These are all very real possibilities, and we have every right to lean into them instead of letting go. But when you start to understand who you are beyond these emotions, it can get easier. When you start to understand that these events and emotions are smaller than the greatness that you are, it can get easier. When you know you have a support system that sees you and loves you unconditionally, even in your most vulnerable moments, it can be easier. When you know you are a beautiful expression of Source Energy, and not just a body, you will know how easy it can be.

Emotional events that provide happy, positive experiences will nurture your energy system and, in turn, help to promote good health in your physical system. If you have an experience that you perceive as an emotionally positive event in which great joy, happiness, or some other positive emotion is created, your body will use this positive energy to its benefit and thrive. There's not much else to it than that! Unfortunately, we will spend a lot more of our focus discussing negative experiences and the importance of working through them compared to this one paragraph on how positive experiences affect us. But that's just the nuts and bolts of it. When everything is good, everything is good. It will (almost) always be your choice to decide what is good and what is not. Remember, no matter what happens to you, you always have a choice, and your choice is how you are going to define who you are within the framework of the events that happen to you.

It's up to you! How will *you* move forward?

An Imbalanced Chakra

Let's suppose when you were a child, your parents never gave you the opportunity to express your thoughts or feelings. Your father ruled with an iron fist, and you were scared to voice your opinions. Your mother had no patience with you and belittled everything you said. Because you feared your father and tried to avoid your mother's snide comments, you chose to never speak your truth. This lack of expression on your part unfortunately became part of your personality into adulthood. Now you find yourself in a relationship with a partner or employer (or both) whom you feel dominated by in terms of communication. Though on the surface you try to appear unaffected by this, on an energetic level your Fifth Chakra (Throat Chakra) is very imbalanced and low on energy. It has been lacking balance for years. It does not have the strength to support the parts of the body it takes care of (throat, thyroid, mouth, teeth, cervical vertebra, jaw, ears, nose). Without a strong Chakra, physical imbalance and disease can follow. The only way to truly overcome the imbalance in this Chakra is to first acknowledge the emotional pain of not being heard as a child, and then you must nurture both who you are as an adult and who you were as a child. Learning to speak your truth and express your feelings is of the utmost importance when healing from such an experience. Sometimes baby steps are necessary. As you start to heal this Chakra it may feel very uncomfortable to speak your truth in front of others, but as you exercise this Chakra and start to express yourself from a place of power, the Chakra will regain balance and any diseases that may have developed can be avoided or healed. A great therapy for healing Chakras is to work with a life coach. A good life coach will guide you by asking the right questions. From there, you will reveal to yourself the truth about how you perceive your experiences. A great life coach will hold up a mirror to you and gently help you see the layers of yourself that brought you to where you are now. It's easy to bury traumas and negative events. Unfortunately, they will always resurface someday, usually in the form of an emotional weakness, physical weakness, or disease.

One summer, my oldest daughter and I binged a very popular series on Netflix, *Call the Midwife*. The first season was based on the real events taken from the diary of the main character of the show. The setting took place in Poplar in London's East End during the late 1950s. The main character, Jenny Lee, was a midwife and nurse to Poplar's residents. Almost all appointments were house calls, so the midwives were able to get to know their patients' personal lives. They tended to midwife duties as well as general health problems. Watching the show with my knowledge of Chakras, I thought the series was amazing. As each episode unfolded, the trials and tribulations of the patients were revealed to the audience, and I could see how the emotional heartaches of each person's life ultimately led to the health issue they suffered from. It was very accurate. I watched love relationships that turned bitter bring on heart attacks. Financial burdens yielded bone and muscle conditions, and rape led to reproductive issues. Movies based in fiction don't have writers who understand how the Chakra system really works, so those story lines don't usually show their characters suffering or dying from the right diseases. *Call the Midwife* was based on real-life events taken from a woman's diary. She intimately knew her patients for years. These people died from diseases that were brought on by Chakra imbalances that matched the hardships they lived through. If you have a passionate interest in Chakras or wish to someday move on from your body in a healthy, peaceful sleep, I highly recommend *Call the Midwife* to get an accurate glimpse of how emotional suffering will lead to disease.

Getting to Know Our New Friends, the Chakras

The Chakra system is an amazing and important system to be aware of within our being because it is so connected to how we interpret each one of our experiences. When first learning about Chakras, it's easier to start slow. Then add a little more and then a little more information. Don't worry. You're doing an absolutely amazing job. Just keep your mind open. As you continue to learn, everything will start to become clear.

Here are some basic characteristics of Chakras to help you start developing a really good relationship with these energy centers.

- A Chakra is an energy vortex (like a tornado). This spinning vortex pulls the energy of your surroundings into you. Whether it's the energy of your own personal event or the energy of the situation of which you are a part, your Chakras will pull that energy in. For example, have you ever felt the energy of a room of people you just walked into? Part of that awareness comes from your Chakras metabolizing the energy. Part of it comes from exercising your sense of feeling.
- Each Chakra governs specific parts of the body. As the Chakra pulls in positive energy, the physical body will be supported and nourished. Negative energy will weaken it.
- Chakras originate in the center of the body and the cone-shaped vortices spin out of the front and the back of the body. The front of your Chakras are designed to react to that which is literally right in front of you. The back side of your Chakras are working with the energy that you want to manifest into your life.
- Balanced Chakras spin clockwise, meaning down on the left side and up on the right side in relation to yourself. Out of balance Chakras spin slowly, counterclockwise, or not at all. They can also feel blocked, muddied, misshapen, oversized, or undersized. It is usually the Chakra balancing

practitioner that feels this, unless you are very in tune with your own Chakras, in which case you will feel something not right. Some people express it as, "I just feel like I'm in a funk." Not wonderfully descriptive, but I get what they mean.

- The information that is pulled in ultimately goes to the nervous system and will energetically support or deplete the parts of the physical body that it governs.
- There are seven main Chakras that correspond to specific endocrine glands.
- The colors of the Chakras follow the same colors of a rainbow or prism, with red starting at the first Chakra. Isn't it interesting that a rainbow can be created by diffracting white light? White light is the energy used when doing energy healing. During energy healing, white light is sent into a person. Depending on what is needed for the individual to heal, the exact color (vibrational frequency) is pulled out of that white light to do whatever healing is necessary.

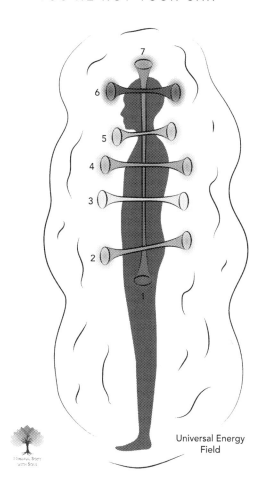

Universal Energy Field

Unfortunately this diagram could not be published in color. Each Chakra illuminates a color that resonates with it. Chapter four will go into greater detail of each Chakra color.

The locations of the Chakras are as follows:

First Chakra

- Base of body, very bottom of body (bottom of torso, not the feet)

- Gland: Adrenals

Second Chakra

- Front: above the pubic bone, below navel
- Back: low back/sacrum area.
- Gland: Ovaries/Testes

Third Chakra

- Front: just below sternum
- Back: mid back/thoracic area
- Gland: Pancreas

Fourth Chakra

- Front: center of chest next to heart
- Back: between the shoulder blades
- Gland: Thymus

Fifth Chakra

- Front: at the thyroid/voice box/trachea
- Back: back of the neck at cervical spine
- Gland: Thyroid

Sixth Chakra

- Front: middle of forehead above eyebrows
- Back: back of the head
- Gland: Pituitary

Seventh Chakra

- Top of the head at crown
- Gland: Pineal

- Notice on the diagram how the first and seventh Chakras don't have front/back locations. This is because the vortex of energy shines downward and upward respectively. The squiggly lines outside the body represent the Universal Energy Field (UEF, which will be discussed in chapter six.)
- Overall, the average human has 114 major and minor Chakras.
- Chakras are the energy centers through which situations and encounters from the world outside of our body filter; as does the UEF, which contains an abundance of information available to us.
- If the Chakras are not spinning clockwise, or otherwise out of balance, the information coming into us will greatly affect how we process, interpret, and ultimately feel about a situation. The quality of the spin is most often directly related to other past experiences. If the Heart Chakra is spinning slowly or not spinning at all, the capacity to love and feel love may be diminished. Often people think if they have a Chakra balancing session they are fixed, and for a time they are. There is much value in having a Chakra balancing session. But once the person gets back to their life and starts having experiences again, the Chakras may quickly fall back out of balance because the person continues to perceive an event the same way as before.

People need to find a way to bring balance to their Chakras and life in general, but there is also the need to process past events and find liberation from the negative feelings that were assigned to that event in the first place. I tell my clients, "It is ok to have an emotional reaction to your experience. In fact, it's important. But once the experience is over, you must leave the emotion in the past along with the experience itself. You will remember the experience, and this is good because from it you gain wisdom. But do not carry around the weight of the pain. Do not relive the pain over and over. Just put it down. Let it go." This is much easier said than done. But first it must be said. Then, we work on making it so.

Think of it in terms of a tight muscle. If you sit at a computer all day and your neck muscles get very tight, a good massage can loosen them up and you feel better. The next few days you're back at your computer, and before you know it, those neck muscles are in a knot once again. To truly heal your neck, you must find a new job that doesn't require sitting at a computer all day! Or you need to learn stretches that will help alleviate the pain, and you need to change the way you interact with your workstation. The latter is most healing because chances are, any job you have will hurt your neck muscles that are now sensitive to becoming tight again. Similarly, someone with an imbalanced Heart Chakra must find a new way to approach love in their life. They must consciously choose to feel love again and want that emotion in their life (or whatever emotional challenge they are having within the Heart Chakra). Realizing why they feel so unloving, unloved, or unlovable is very helpful, because it is the first step to allowing them to finally leave that emotion in the past where it belongs and focus on their positive aspects. Keep in mind though, every emotion and every situation is convoluted with twists and turns. When it comes to how we feel about things, nothing is straightforward. The one thing that is certain, though, is that awareness is the first step toward actualization.

Here are some fun facts to help you become better acquainted with the part of yourself you never knew:

- We have secondary Chakras on the palms of our hands to take in information as we navigate the world through touch exploration. Everything we touch is energy even if it's a physical thing. Hand Chakras absorb energy while holding on to an object or if the hand just grazes over it.

- The breasts (more specifically the nipples) each have a secondary Chakra that are meant to interact with newborns as they nurse. The newborn Chakra system is not highly developed at birth, and nipple Chakras help babies absorb the energy they need to flourish. Nipple Chakras infuse breast milk with energy needed by the growing baby. For those who have high psychic perception, a baby nursing or laying her head on her mother's breast would look like a beautiful flow of energy going from mother to child. Also, the more balanced these Chakras are, the more sexually sensitive the nipples will be.

- Secondary Chakras are also found on the bottoms of the feet to help absorb very important, very powerful earth energy. If you tend to feel out of balance or separated from your body, going barefoot is a beautiful thing! It will help you to stay connected to the earth and keep your complete energy system firmly rooted into the body.

- In addition to the seven main Chakras, there are two more main Chakras that get very little attention. Both are located off the body and connected to us through our auric field. One of them is called the Earth Star Chakra and is located below the level of our feet so it spends most of its time under the ground. It is used like a drain to consciously move out unwanted energies, like a drain in a bathroom shower. As the water cleanses the body, all the dirt and debris wash away down the drain. The Earth Star Chakra can be thought of in a similar way. Through meditation, unwanted energies can be intentionally released and moved out of the energy system through this Chakra. From here the energy will travel back into the Universe, where it can be quickly recycled into more usable, positive energy.

- The other lesser known Chakra is located off the body above the Crown Chakra and is called the Lunar Chakra. It connects with the powerful energy of the moon. As we know, the moon is responsible for many cycles in nature and has a power over the ocean. Moon energy awakens the goddess energy within us (regardless of your gender). This Chakra is like an antenna that reels in that energy and allows us to connect with feminine power. The moon's energy will follow the intention you set. Folklore says a full moon can fill up the asylums and make a cat act a little nutty. But if you intend for moonlight to provide a calm, cooling energy, that is what will transcend. Irritable feelings can also be defused when holding a positive intention in moonlight. At night, lay outside or near a window to absorb its power. Crystals become especially charged in moonlight, so lay them on or near you as you bask in the magic of the moon.

- Resonating vibrations from singing bowls can open blocked Chakras. Sound is the number-one best way to clear energy within a room, within yourself, and within your Chakras. Do not play singing bowls within five feet of a pregnant woman. The sounds of the bowls vibrating within the amniotic fluid is very intense and can be stressful for a delicate fetus.

- The entrance and exit point into and out of the body is always through the Crown Chakra, whether the Soul is entering a new body or exiting an expired body. It is important for the Soul to have the opportunity to get used to being in a body when it's preparing for another incarnation. When we are in energy form, there is no such thing as physical limitations, so getting used to the body as the fetus is growing is something the Soul does by way of the Crown Chakra (once the body starts to develop a Chakra system.) The Soul travels in and out of the body from here.

- The health of all Chakras is completely related to emotions and the information taken in by that Chakra. What you experience *and how you choose to perceive it* will directly affect your health.
- When a person's Chakra is too closed or out of balance, the person will sometimes (but not always) dislike the color of that Chakra. They will say it's their least favorite color, won't wear the color, and have adverse feelings toward the color. When the person is ready to heal a particular Chakra or it starts to come back into balance, it will suddenly become their favorite color!
- Personalities may also be a clue to an imbalanced Chakra. Here is a short list to give you an idea of personality traits from imbalanced Chakras:

– Feeling like the victim	– Unable to relax
– Being a bully	– Overly indulgent
– Being a controller	– Being a sexual deviant
– Lacking motivation	– Lacking confidence
– Having many fears	– Having no sense of self
– Talking in excess	– Putting up "walls"
– Fear of dying	– Unconcerned about others
– Overly analytical	– Lacking compassion

- There are many yoga poses that help to bring balance back into Chakras. If you do a pose for a specific Chakra, you will also be directly helping the body parts that are governed by that Chakra. Chapter four will deconstruct each Chakra to help you get a clear picture of the whole system, right down to which foods, crystals, yoga poses, and activities will benefit each one.
- Your mind, body, Soul, and Chakras all function together. They are a network of "bosses," each overseeing their own special enterprise. Each one is only as strong as the weakest

"boss." They all have "managers," "sub-managers," and "workers" who contribute to the overall success of your entire being. During the time you are in your human body, your entire being *is* your mind, body, Soul, and Chakras. Your Soul, however, is the true essence of who you are forever.

• An easy way to determine which of your Chakras is out of balance is to determine which of your body parts seems to always get sick. Do you have a weak part of your body? What are your physical ailments? Figure out which Chakra governs this body part(s). It is probably the Chakra that is out of balance.

THREE

VIBRATIONAL FREQUENCY, EASIER THAN YOU THINK

Good Vibrations

When our body's overall vibrational frequency is low, we tend to have low feelings. We are tired, sad, mad, anxious, depressed, irritated, uninterested, or just plain blah. It's hard to accomplish our goals, and even our bodies can feel more painful. Mentally and emotionally, we tend to feel more confusion. Being around others can feel very challenging. Overall, life seems very bleak and like a chore. This is a perfect recipe for arguments to start bubbling.

When our vibrational frequency is higher, we tend to feel energized and enlightened. Mentally and emotionally, we have a greater sense of clarity, and life feels good. We instantly begin to feel more joy, love, peace, and inner power. We feel more natural and being in the company of others can make us feel more complete. Creating what we want in our life becomes easier. We start to notice synchronicities, and we move through life with ease. Life feels very good when our vibrational frequency is high. Life feels as good as it was meant to feel, much like driving down the highway in the proper gear feels good. If your car was stuck in neutral or low gear, driving down the highway would feel very wrong. You say to yourself, *Yeah, I'm doing this but something's not right. My car is not moving along as it should and that is making me feel so stressed!* Then, once you slip it back into the proper gear, your little car rides smoothly again, balance is back, and you're singing along with the music.

Everything in the Universe is energy and everything in the Universe vibrates. Our own bodies vibrate at a specific frequency, and each part of our bodies vibrates with its own vibrational frequencies. Organs each vibrate at their own rate. Bones vibrate at a different frequency than organs, and each bone and muscle vibrates differently from the others. Our cells also vibrate. And the cells of your brain are vibrating at a different frequency than the cells of your heart. Chakras have a vibrational frequency that differ from the frequencies of our physical body.

Some energy bodies in the Universe have the same or similar vibrational frequencies to each other, and this makes them very attracted to each other. The Law of Attraction allows for things that are alike to be attracted to each other. (Check out the Glossary for more on Law of Attraction and Vibrations.)

For example, the Root Chakra has vibrational attraction to:

- The sound resonated by the musical note F
- Stones and crystals
  - red calcite, bloodstone
  - hematite
  - smokey quartz
  - garnet
  - ruby
  - agate
  - black tourmaline

- Foods
  - protein
  - legumes
  - beans
  - root vegetables
  - cayenne pepper
  - horseradish

Because these rocks, foods, and the note F match the vibrational frequency (VF) of the Root Chakra, they will help to support the Root Chakra, especially when it is out of balance. Similarly, when you do activities, think thoughts, and live your life in a way that resonates with what you want to create for yourself, you are supporting the outcome because these all resonate with the same vibrational frequency of what you're trying to attract. This is directly related to the Law of Attraction. What you're trying to attract is more Universal Energy that vibrates at the same rate as what you want.

When you raise your own VF, the energy at your disposal is more powerful and your ability to create is amplified. There are ways to raise your VF, some of which you probably do on a regular basis and don't even realize it. But you do probably notice how good you feel during and after you engage in these activities. Here are some great ways to raise your own vibrational frequency.

Raise It Up!

Sing

Singing is a very fast and easy way to raise your frequency, especially if you sing songs that have a special meaning to you or that you feel you sing especially well. So, sing loud and sing proud! Remember, true beauty lies in the eye of the beholder, and beautiful singing lies in the ear of the listener. Be confident in your singing! But if it makes you more comfortable to do this alone, go to a private place where you know your ears will be the only ears around. Then sing at the top of your lungs. Belt it out. You're going to feel great! And as you raise your vibration, you will also be doing wonderful things for your Throat Chakra. (Your car is a great place to sing privately, by the way.)

Listen to or play music

Whether you are singing, listening to music, playing music, absorbing the vibrations of a Tibetan singing bowl sound bath, or

JENNIFER MERRITTS

simply chiming a bell, music clears and raises energy. Sound will very efficiently clear the energy in a room or around yourself. Get creative with your music and just enjoy it. If you or a loved one struggles with a cognitive or learning disability, music therapy is a marvelous way to take back your health. Music Therapy is not new, but it has gotten more and more exposure in recent years. Do some research on it, because this may be exactly what you or your loved one needs to find peace. Making and creating music will also help boost the Sacral Chakra, which is the Chakra involved with creativity.

Move your body

Walk, sway, dance, exercise, or do yoga or tai chi. They all move your energy and help the stagnated energy flow better. As your blood starts moving, your hormones start moving. Remember, earlier we said that hormones are directly related to your Chakras. Movement also helps lymph flow through your lymphatic system, which is responsible for cleansing the inside of your body. In fact, it's the only way to get the lymph moving (unless you have a lymphatic massage). Try playing tribal drum music and just let your body move with the beat. Don't worry about doing special dance steps. Just move! While doing this you'll also be reconnecting your body to the earth and feel your Root Chakra wake up!

Laugh

Laughter really is the best medicine, especially belly laughs. Find humor in your situation. Let go of the seriousness of everything, and just laugh about it for a moment. Picture your own life as a comedy on TV. If you can't laugh, fake it! And keep faking it until it starts to feel real. If you're with someone else and they hear you trying to fake laugh, they're going to start laughing too and the contagiousness of it

— 50 —

takes off! You'll see it can build up to some good stuff! Find humor on TV, at a stand-up comedy show, when you're with your friends, and when you watch adorable animal videos. You can even find humor in the craziness of our world. Might as well laugh because the other option is to get angry. Neither will fix the situation, but laughing will fix you! It will also positively affect your Heart and Solar Plexus Chakras.

Meditate

This is great for all the Chakras. Meditating raises your vibrational frequency to a point that makes it easy for you to connect with Spirit and Source, loved ones who have passed, and your Guides and Angels. It gives you access to the information you seek. Your Third Eye Chakra will become very activated as well. (This Chakra is where you start to develop your "clairs," like clairvoyance, clairsentience, and claircognizence.) When you meditate, you connect your Soul's light with Source Light. As you stay in this meditative state, and do diaphragmatic breathing, the parasympathetic system kicks in, and healing energy fills your entire being. It is now scientifically known that meditating can change cell health *and* improve mood. Meditating not only can increase your VF, but it can also make you healthier! Why on earth are you *not* doing it? If your mind wanders while you practice, let it! Then, without judgment against yourself, bring your attention back to your meditation. Experiment with different methods of mediation so you know which one is best for you. Make it a routine in your day. (Before bed will probably put you to sleep. For some people, that can be a good thing!) You can also create a ritual while meditating, using candles, incense, music, a water fountain, etc. I've started writing a mini-book called *OMM—Open Minded Meditation*. It's a great tool for beginners.

Be in nature

An amazing way to stay grounded and to raise your vibration is to get in the dirt! There is nothing more basic and real than being in nature. Whether it's hiking at Yosemite or sitting on a quiet corner of earth at your city park, you will feel recharged after absorbing the powerful energy our world provides. You can buy an earthing mat if you can't find a place to root into actual nature, but actual nature is available, free, and beautiful! Go get yourself some of that. Your Root Chakra will benefit as you connect to mother earth.

Water

Not only does water nourish and support the Sacral Chakra, this element is an incredible vibrational frequency raiser. Why do children love water so much? Because they intuitively know how good it is for their Souls. Our bodies are made up of mostly water, so of course being in the energy of water is going to make us feel very relaxed and happy. Water is also a conductor of energy. Energy moves swiftly and easily through water, which is why it is so important to stay well hydrated when focusing on your energy system. Swim in it. Take a shower. Take a bath. Sit by a stream. Paddle down a river. Play in the ocean waves. Get soaked in a rainstorm. Float in a pond. Run through puddles. Go snorkeling. Walk on the beach and get your feet wet. Skip rocks. Have a water balloon fight. Drink lots of it. Water! Just do it!

Sleep

When you're completely exhausted, run down, and overworked, you must sleep to recharge all parts of your physical and energetic bodies. Being rested will also help you make better decisions. Having your wits about you will stop you from doing things that lower your vibrational frequency if you find yourself going down the proverbial "dark path." Going to sleep will also put an end to any negative thinking you have been doing. When you wake up, fresh and energized, your situation usually looks much brighter. Sleeping is the time your body uses to repair and heal, but sometimes we experience insomnia for a few nights or much longer. We all know some of the obvious things to do to fall asleep easier. Shut off the blue screens at least an hour before bed, don't eat at least two or three hours before bed, make your room dark, and block all the lights that come out of electronics. If you do these things but you still can't shut off the monkey mind, try closing your eyes and see/think of a black dot on a white background. See how long you can hold this image in your awareness. Focusing on just one thing like this can help quiet the brain and let sleep take over. Another idea that works for almost everyone is to do parasympathetic breathing, also known as belly breathing or diaphragmatic breathing. To do this simply take deep, slow inhales and exhales. Make your inhale be at least to the count of four Mississippi's and your exhale at least five Mississippi's. On every inhale be sure to let your belly expand and inflate, on every exhale let your belly relax. Breathing like this activates your parasympathetic system which is the part of your nervous system that lets you relax, rest, and repair. If this still isn't helping, find a good naturopath or acupuncturist who can help you with sleep. Everyone deserves a good night's rest. Sleep deprivation can feel like torture. It's going to be very hard to raise your vibration without sleep.

Cleanse your energy with breath

When we meditate there is much emphasis on breathing. Not only is it a focus point to help quiet our minds, but it also allows stagnated energy to start moving. It can be helpful to think of breath as the current that carries energy as we kick-start our connection to white light. Every Chakra is affected by focused, intentional breath. There are many types of breathing. See which one works best for you.

- Ujjayi Breathing (lowers heart rate, improves thyroid, calms NS, increases concentration) Sometimes called ocean breathing or Darth Vader breathing.
- Alternate Nostril Breathing (lowers heart rate, calms NS, increases energy, balances parasympathetic system)
- Belly Breathing (activates the parasympathetic system). Also known as diaphragmatic breathing.

Say affirmations, mantras, prayers

Not only does this raise your vibrational frequency, saying affirmations will also balance and strengthen your Crown Chakra. Writing your own affirmations and saying them can immediately start to make you feel better. Hearing yourself say the positive outcome to a problem gives you a life raft to hold on to. The more you say it, the bigger the life raft gets until you are firmly standing on dry land, confident and happy. Write them down on sticky notes and stick them everywhere! The more often you bring the thought into your conscious awareness, the more of that vibrational frequency you are attracting toward yourself. Remember the Law of Attraction. If you want something, think about it more than you think about its negative opposite. You can even start to change the story that you tell about yourself and to yourself. Whether you're thinking internally or telling someone else, change the commentary. This doesn't mean you should flat-out lie about your situation but do try to tell a more positive story. One that centers on the good things in your life. When you find yourself choosing words like "It's miserable," "I'm so sad," "business is slow," try choosing these words instead: "I'm doing great! I'm focusing on happiness. Business is getting better and better!" Soon your entire narrative about yourself will change, allowing positive energy to infiltrate your whole life. How drastically you change your story is up to you.

Learn to balance your Chakras

There are many ways to do this. Tibetan singing bowls will balance your Chakras very nicely. Find a sound bath in your area. Listen to guided meditations that focus on Chakra balancing. Imagine the brilliant color of each Chakra illuminating the space it occupies in and around you. With intention, bring white light (by way of your breath) to each Chakra. Start to visualize each of your Chakras clear and full of its color, spinning strongly. Unpack the emotions that you store in each Chakra. If you need help sorting them out, get a life coach to help you affectively dissolve these emotions. The more you are aware of your Chakras, the more you will be able to keep them balanced. Going forward, know that as you encounter emotional challenges it is important to feel the emotion, process the emotion, understand the emotion, accept the emotion, and let go of the emotion. From there, you are left with the memory. Memories are important to keep and will not create a Chakra imbalance. Let go of emotions by letting them stay in the past with the event that created them. Chakras are a part of our body, just like the heart and lungs are a part of the body. An awareness of them is your first step to keeping them healthy. Know them, care about them, and love them as you do the rest of your body.

Be grateful

Find things to be grateful for. If you can't think of anything substantial, start with small things. Here are some examples:

- I'm so grateful my car started this morning.
- I'm grateful for the shade coming from this magnificent tree.

- I'm grateful I have one clean fork left in my silverware drawer to eat my dinner with.
- I'm grateful that bird poop did not land in my hair.

Get out your pen and paper and write a minimum of ten things. As you start writing, you're going to find more and more things to be grateful for. Try to dig deep. Family, money, and health are really good things to be grateful for, but what else? There really is so much more! When you are grateful, you get a warm and fuzzy feeling inside. That's your vibration starting to rise.

Journal

Journaling can be very therapeutic and can be a record of how far you've come. Use paper notebooks or use journaling software. Journaling can lead you to solutions. Solutions vibrate much more highly than problems. Write down all the things that make you feel mad, sad, disappointed, etc. Get these feelings out of your mind and onto paper. Sometimes getting them out of the mind lessens the mental load a little bit. You may also start to see them in a different light. A light that shines on the answers, perhaps. Or a light that makes them seem smaller. This helps you process your thoughts and can be very therapeutic. Go deep and find those heavy emotions that have spiked their thorns into the depths of your energetic being. Bring them to the surface as you write and allow those prickly emotions and memories to move into the past where they belong. Let them go. Let them merge back to the event from which they came. Don't carry them with you forever. You can remember your past, but you don't have to endlessly feel the pain. Journaling can help remove emotional pain and stress. (Remember, emotional burdens and stress are two things that will ultimately manifest into a physical disease). Looking at your problems on paper can sometimes make the problems seem less daunting. Even more powerful is screaming them out loud on top of a mountain, and I mean really screaming them! If it's anxiety about a future event that's anchoring its spikes into you, remember this: What we worry about rarely happens. But if it does, seldom do we experience it as traumatically and dramatically as what we imagined.

Release

Releasing emotions can help you purge the internal pollutants that can create imbalances within any Chakra. It's so easy for someone to say to someone else, "just let it go." But *how* do you let it go? Some solutions may work for some of us, but all solutions do not work for all of us. With that in mind, here is an exercise you can try that may help you release. Get a picture of the person or thing that has created disharmony in your life. It will be the person or thing that you are having very negative emotions toward. If you don't have a picture, anything that you feel is a representation of it will work just fine. Set aside five to ten minutes of quiet, private time for yourself. No distractions. In that time, say how you feel, express the chaos that has stormed into your life as a result of this person or thing. Let yourself really express on the outside how you're feeling on the inside. Identify what that emotion is. Is it rage? Sadness? Disappointment? Confusion? Disdain? Humiliation? Abandonment? Deception? Now let it out! Scream, yell, cry, don't hold back! Express how you really feel. Let your whole body get involved. By looking at the picture of the person or thing that created your pain, you will be connecting with their energy without feeling the weight of their negative energy. Know that as you release the physical energy by acting out, you are also releasing emotional energy that has been harbored within your entire being for a long time. You can do this as many times as you like to fully purge and release. But don't let it consume your whole day. Five to ten minutes each time you do this exercise is all you need. Then fill yourself with positive vibrations by picking one of the other activities on this list.

Help others

What a great way to raise your vibration! When others feel good about the help they are receiving, that energy is then projected on to you. The feeling is fabulous. What is done to one of us is done to all of us. The help you give to others doesn't have to be elaborate. Little acts of kindness raise vibrations immensely. See how many you can do in a day and record it on your phone. Each day try to do one more than the last day. Be the blessing in someone else's life. This will help support many Chakras, especially your Heart and Solar Plexus Chakras.

Forgive

Carrying grief, anger, and hate is very heavy. It only hurts *you* to continue with that hate or grief. It does not necessarily hurt the other person. Sometimes the other person is completely unaware of how much pain you have. Or they really don't care. Your Heart Chakra will suffer the most when you hold on to these things. Leave hurt in the past where it happened. As Nelson Mandela said, "Hating someone is like drinking poison and expecting the other person to die from it." If you choose to harbor what pains you, that is your choice, and it is your choice to send it away. How many times will you run barefoot through broken glass before you choose not to do it anymore? All your choices can be that easy, you just have to view them from a new perspective. Holding onto a grudge or anger is very heavy and exhausting to do. Instead, send Love Energy to your enemy and feel your vibrational frequency go up!

Feel Love

Imagine Love Energy being sent out to the people you want to send positive high-vibrating energy to. Connect your thoughts and awareness with Source or the Universe and imagine white light coming into your Crown Chakra. Be aware of this light bathing you and all your Chakras. Then, using your intention, send that love to anyone you think can benefit from it. You can even keep it for yourself. Know that there is no wrong way to do this, no secret steps to follow. Just intend for it to happen, and it will. After channeling Love Energy for yourself, start to compliment yourself. Focus on the parts of you that you really like. Start with that cute little freckle you've always admired on your toe and continue from there. Know that your uniqueness is absolutely gorgeous. The part of you that is different from everyone else is not your worst part. It is your most amazing part! Feel confident in your uniqueness. Your confidence and love for yourself will be the power that changes the currents of the stream.

Put down your device

Just put it down. You know what I mean. Put it down and go live in the real world. Make your own experiences and stop watching other people's experiences. Vibrate with the natural world! Exist in the here and now!

Which of these exercises resonates with you most? Do you have other exercises you already do that work for you?

Try them all and see which ones make you feel the best.

Do at least one of these per day. The more you do high vibrational things the better you are going to feel. But even if you only do them once in a while, it's better than not doing them at all.

What if everyone on the planet did something to make themselves happy and vibrate at a higher frequency every day? What could our world be like? Can you start the ball rolling? Can you be the change you seek? Pass on your good vibrations to others and share high-vibrating ideas with others. Make it happen, you can do it!

FOUR

THE DECONSTRUCTED CHAKRAS AND THEN SILENCE

The Deconstructed Root Chakra

First Chakra—Root Chakra
Sanskrit name: Muladhara
Meaning: root or support
Location: base of spine, bottom of body (pelvic floor), and last three vertebrae (L5, sacrum, coccyx)
Color: red

Main focus: survival/physical needs

Gland: adrenals

Developmental age: birth to seven years

Associated sense: stillness with the earth and sense of smell

Element: Earth

Musical Note: F

Supporting stones: red calcite, bloodstone, hematite, smokey quartz, garnet, ruby, agate, black tourmaline

Supporting foods: protein, legumes, beans, root vegetables, cayenne pepper, horseradish

Governs: bones, blood, colon, legs, feet

Has to do with feeling safe in the world, feeling connected to the earth and your family/people/tribe. Knowing you have a good job, enough food, money, a safe home to live in

Physical Dysfunctions: osteoporosis, bone abnormalities, bone cancer, Crohn's disease, colon issues, sacral spine issues, lower back/leg/feet issues, constipation, incontinence, weight gain, weight loss, eating disorders

Emotional Dysfunctions: fears, anxiety, nightmares, eating disorders, feeling stuck, distractibility, inability to take action

Archetypes: mother earth (functional), victim (dysfunctional)

When this Chakra is too open, individuals will appear to be overly materialistic, bullying, and self-centered. They act before they think.

When this Chakra is too closed, individuals will seem emotionally needy and self-destructive, have low self-esteem, and will seem fearful.

When energy flows freely in this Chakra, individuals will feel grounded within themselves as well as with the world around them. They will have high physical energy and will demonstrate self-mastery. They are not worriers.

How to Balance Muladhara (Root Chakra)

Yoga Poses:

1. Pavanamuktasna—Knee to Chest Pose
2. Janu Sirsansana—Head to Knee Pose
3. Padmasana—Lotus or Half Lotus Pose
4. Malasana—Squatting Pose
5. Mula Bandha—Contraction of pelvic floor (not buttocks or anus), similar to Kegels
6. Virabhadrasana I—Warrior 1 Pose
7. Tadasana—Mountain Pose
8. Utkatasana—Chair Pose

Meditate

Bring your awareness to the Root Chakra. Using your mind's eye, visualize the brilliant color red. As you inhale, use your intention to breathe in red light, and then watch it make its way into the Root Chakra.

Move Your Body

In the privacy of your room, play some rhythmic drumming music (easy to find on YouTube). Feel the beat of the drums enter your body and start to move with the beat. If you feel balanced, close your eyes and just let the beat of the music move you around. This is also beneficial for the Sacral Chakra. (Try shamanic drum and steel drum music.)

Chanting, Toning Sounds, or Music

Sounds create vibrations in the body, and these vibrations help the cells rebalance their energy for optimal functioning. Sound will balance your Chakras and clear the energy in a room.

- Chanting: The word LAM resonates with the Root Chakra. Say LLLAAAMMM as if the sound is coming from your Root. Try getting a deep, low sound like a monk chanting in a monastery. Be mindful to say each sound. L, A, M. The A sound has a tiny hint of O to it. So when you are sounding the A, make your lips into a circle while still saying AAAAA. Take a deep breath and say the chant for as long as your breath will allow. (LAM rhymes with the man's name Tom.)
- Toning sounds: Tibetan or Himalayan singing bowls. Any instrument that plays the note F resonates with Root Chakra.
- Music: Any music that makes you feel good. After all, that's the goal, right? *Feeling good*!

Bring anything into your auric field or personal space that resonates with the same frequency as the Chakra you are focused on. For Root Chakra: eat, wear, surround yourself with red. Sit on the earth, play in the dirt, walk barefoot, smell the flowers. Change the story that you tell about yourself. Start telling a new and positive story about your family, finances, security, and support system.

The Deconstructed Sacral Chakra

Second Chakra—Sacral Chakra
Sanskrit name: Svadhisthana
Meaning: sweetness
Location: between navel and genitals—lower abdomen
Color: orange
Main focus: Finding pleasure and overall enjoyment of life. Also tied to sexuality and creativity.
Gland: ovaries/testes
Developmental age: seven to fourteen years
Associated sense: feeling emotions and sense of taste
Element: water
Musical note: C
Supporting stones: orange calcite, citrine, carnelian, tiger's eye
Supporting foods: liquids, oranges, melon, pumpkin, squash, sweet potato, turmeric

Governs: reproductive organs, bladder, lumbar vertebrae, large intestine, prostate, kidneys, lymph system

Has to do with sexuality, creativity, and a zest for life. This Chakra also deals with overindulgence and underindulgence and finding the balance between work and play.

Physical dysfunctions: female/male reproductive issues, impotence, low libido, large intestine issues, bladder issues, urinary incontinence, UTI, pain during intercourse, complications with kidneys, low back pain, lymphatic swelling

Emotional dysfunctions: unbalanced sex drive, instability, creative slump, gluttony, inability to have fun

Archetypes: sovereign (functional), martyr (dysfunctional)

When this Chakra is too open, individuals will appear emotionally unbalanced, manipulative, and sexually addictive. Sex and sexual references seem to dominate their lives. They have gluttonous tendencies.

When this Chakra is too closed, individuals will seem oversensitive and be hard on themselves. They feel like a victim, have feelings of guilt for unfounded reasons, and are frigid or impotent. They do not have a balance of enjoyment in life.

When this Chakra is balanced, individuals will be trusting, expressive, attuned to their feelings, creative, and comfortable expressing themselves sexually. They are able to sit within the depths of their emotions with ease and peace. They easily express needs and emotions and know how to set healthy boundaries with others.

How to Balance Svadhisthana (Sacral Chakra)

Yoga Poses

1. Seated Pelvic Circles—Sitting crossed legged or half lotus, place your hands on your knees and make circles with your

torso. Focus on your Sacral Chakra and imagine it as the pivot point.

2. Baddha konasana—Butterfly pose with forward fold
3. Bhujangasana—Cobra Pose
4. Utkata Konasana—Goddess Pose
5. Anjaneyasana—Low Lunge, hands on floor
6. Supta Vajrasana—Reclined Thunderbolt Pose
7. Ashta Chandrasana—Crescent Pose
8. Utthita Trikonasana—Triangle Pose

Meditate

Bring your awareness to the Sacral Chakra. Using your mind's eye, visualize the brilliant color orange. As you inhale, use your intention to breathe in orange light, and then watch it make its way into the Sacral Chakra.

Be Creative

The Sacral Chakra's greatest creation is procreation. But this Chakra's creativity is not limited to only making babies. Create anything you desire. That includes baking, gardening, writing, journaling, decorating, painting, and even making a toothpick sculpture!

Be Silly

Many of us, especially women, have an underdeveloped Sacral Chakra. As children we were told to stay away from our private parts and stay away from sex. Many generations were told the most basic human instinct (sexual contact) was inappropriate. We were encouraged to follow what society was doing, which was to work hard and not overindulge. If you want to heal your Sacral Chakra, it's time to get silly. Have fun and enjoy the process. Take time to figure out what makes you happy.

Chanting, Toning Sounds, and Water

- Chanting: The word VAM resonates with Sacral Chakra. Say VVVAAAMMM as if the sound is coming from your Sacrum. Follow the same instructions for LAM and Root Chakra.
- Toning Sounds: Tibetan or Himalayan singing bowls. Any instrument that plays the note C resonates with Sacral Chakra.
- Swim in the water, especially clean, natural water like a lake or the ocean. The Sacral Chakra element is water. There is nothing more powerful and healing than hours spent in this splendidly restoring and soothing element to awaken and mend your Sacral Chakra. Except, of course, swimming in natural water while moonlight shines on you!

Note: This can promote surprising orgasms.

The Deconstructed Solar Plexus Chakra

Third Chakra—Solar Plexus Chakra
Sanskrit name: Manipura
Meaning: lustrous gem of the land
Location: between navel and base of sternum—upper abdomen
Color: yellow
Main focus: personal power/self will
Gland: pancreas
Developmental age: fourteen to twenty-one years
Associated sense: Knowing oneself (seeing oneself)
Element: fire
Musical note: G
Supporting stones: yellow citrine, yellow labradorite, yellow calcite, sunstone, yellow cat's eye
Supporting foods: spices with heat (only for under active Chakra), healthy carbohydrates like brown rice, oats, quinoa, buckwheat, bananas, and chickpeas
Governs: small intestine, stomach, diaphragm, metabolism, muscles, pancreas, liver, spleen

Has to do with personal power, self-esteem, knowing who you are and what your path is in the world. Being confident in yourself, but with grace and kindness.

Physical dysfunctions: issues with stomach, pancreas, liver, gallbladder, small intestine, diabetes, digestive issues, inability to absorb nutrients, muscle development, weight fluctuations

Emotional dysfunctions: controlling, aggressive, incapable of empathy, addictive personality, conceited, oversensitive, low self-esteem, meek

Archetypes: spiritual warrior (functional), servant (dysfunctional)

When this Chakra is too open, individuals will appear to be angry, controlling, workaholics, judgmental, and superior.

When this Chakra is too closed, individuals will be overly concerned by what others think, lack confidence, need constant reassurance, and be unable to take control. They will be passive followers and feel excessively shy.

When this Chakra is balanced, individuals will be able to easily fall into a leadership role while still respecting others. They propel themselves through life like confident warriors, but are still capable of being kind to others.

How to Balance Manipura (Solar Plexus Chakra)

Yoga Poses

1. Tadasana—Mountain Pose (hands in prayer position at Third Chakra, feeling the energy firing up within)
2. Virabhadrasana 1—Warrior 1 Pose
3. Adho Mukha Svanasana/Dandasana—Down Dog to Plank, Plank to Down Dog, repeat.
4. Ardha Matsyandrasana—Half Lord of the Fishes Pose (Seated spinal twist)
5. Paripurna Navasana—Boat Pose

6. Virabhadrasana II—Warrior 2 Pose
7. Surya Mudra—Sun Mudra (very basic yet effective)

Meditate

Bring your awareness to the Solar Plexus Chakra. Using your mind's eye, visualize the brilliant color yellow. As you inhale, use your intention to breathe in yellow light, and then watch it make its way into the Solar Plexus Chakra. It can be helpful to create an altar. Place items on it that resonate with the Chakra you are focused on or fill it with things that represent all Chakras. Other symbolic items can be things that bring a sense of spirituality to your awareness. There are no wrong ideas for your altar.

Take Advice from Eleanor Roosevelt and Her Quotes

- "No one can make you feel inferior without your consent."
- "A woman is like a tea bag: you never know how strong it is until it gets into hot water."
- "Do one thing every day that scares you."
- "You gain strength, courage, and confidence by every experience in which you really stop to look fear in the face. You are able to say to yourself, 'I have lived through this horror. I can take the next that comes along.' You must do the thing you think you cannot do."

Warmth and Laughter

- When your body is warm, it is much easier to activate your Solar Plexus Chakra. Move around, exercise, get warmed up.
- Laughter is so healing for this Chakra because when you are laughing you are constantly thrusting your diaphragm,

which is located right next to your Third Chakra and pancreas. It's like a very vigorous massage for both.

Chanting, Toning Sounds, and Breath of Fire

- Chanting: The word RAM resonates with Solar Plexus Chakra. Say RRRAAAMMM as if the sound is coming from your Solar Plexus. See Root Chakra notes for complete instruction.
- Toning sounds: Tibetan or Himalayan singing bowls. Any instrument that plays the note G resonates with Solar Chakra.
- Breath of Fire Breathing: This aids digestion and increases metabolism.
- Move through the world like you are Freddie Mercury, with complete and unapologetic confidence while still showing care and compassion to others.

The Deconstructed Heart Chakra

Fourth Chakra—Heart Chakra
Sanskrit name: Anahata
Meaning: unstruck; sound that is made without any two things striking. Also means "Place where no hurt exists."
Location: center of chest—next to heart

Color: green with pink at the very center (vibrates the added frequency of pink only when it is balanced and there is a strong spiritual connection to Source)

Main focus: Love for self, for others, for Source (god/goddess spirit, creator) as well as compassion, empathy, and forgiveness for self and others

Gland: thymus

Developmental age: twenty-one to twenty-eight years

Associated sense: loving (and touch)

Element: Air (air, like Love, is within and all around us)

Musical note: D

Supporting stones: green calcite, rose quartz, malachite, jade, watermelon tourmaline

Supporting foods: green leafy vegetables, rose tea, chocolate, red wine (actually, cacao and grapes, but what the heck, let's just say chocolate and red wine)

Governs: heart, chest, breasts, lungs, thoracic spine, circulation, thymus, lymphatic system

Has to do with loving yourself, those around you, and that which is greater than yourself. Having an understanding that you cannot find love outside of yourself until you first find love within yourself. Realizing self-love is much greater than the love given and controlled by another.

Physical dysfunctions: health problems around the lungs, heart, breasts, thoracic spine, thymus gland, shallow breathing, asthma, heart disease, breast cancer, fibrocystic breasts, upper back/shoulder problems

Emotional dysfunctions: codependency, loneliness, melancholy, fears around commitment/betrayal, putting up "walls," problems with jealousy and hatred, unable to keep healthy relationships, narcissism

Archetypes: lover (functional) performer, loner (dysfunctional)

When this Chakra is too open, individuals will seem possessive and overly dramatic. They love conditionally and withhold emotionally to punish.

When this Chakra is too closed, individuals will fear rejection, feel unworthy to receive love, be self-pitying, isolate themselves, feel lonely, and fear intimacy.

When this Chakra is balanced, individuals will be compassionate, love unconditionally (themselves and others), and nurturing. They will be able to be alone without feeling lonely, desire a spiritual experience in lovemaking, and have a relationship with that which is higher than themselves. They are able to forgive and accept those around them, themselves, and their bodies. Love is free flowing regardless of the situation.

How to Balance Anahata (Heart Chakra)

Yoga Poses

1. Urdhva Dhanurasana—Wheel Pose
2. Anuvittasana—Standing Back Bend
3. Anjaneyasana—Low Lunge (hands bound behind back and chin lifted)
4. Matsyandrasana—Fish Pose (with or without bolster behind shoulder blades)
5. Salamba Bhujangasana—Sphinx Pose
6. Bhugangasana—Cobra Pose
7. Sarvangasana—Queen Pose
8. Halasana—Plow Pose

Meditate

Bring your awareness to the Heart Chakra. Using your mind's eye, visualize the brilliant color green. As you inhale, use your intention to breathe in green light, then watch it make its way into the Heart Chakra. You may also do this visualization using pink light.

Forgive, Laugh, Love, Let Go

Forgive: To be fully transcended into your Heart Chakra, you must invoke forgiveness. The Heart Chakra is a place where no hurt exists. When you forgive, you free yourself from the pain that only you can feel and only you can release.

Laugh: Laughing stimulates the Heart Chakra as the air bounces in and out of our lungs. It is hard to house negative feelings in the body when we laugh.

Love: Find something wonderful about everything you do, everyone you meet, and everything you see. Even if it is the tiniest detail of the overall subject, focus on that one positive thing and forget the rest.

Let go: Letting go of that which does not serve you is as easy as making a choice. Choose joy, love, happiness. Let go of fear, hatred, pride, and your ego. It's always your choice.

Tell your story differently. Does your story sound something like this?

- I am sad because ...
- I have a hard time with ...
- I can't do that because ...
- I feel bad when ...
- I have so many problems, and I'll tell you about them all.
- You disappoint me because ...
- You never notice me when ...
- The world is a miserable place to be.

Try telling your story from a loving, positive perspective.

- It makes me happy when ...
- It makes me happy to have ...
- I love it that I can ...
- I feel happy you are ...

- I have so many things to be grateful for, and I'll tell you about them all.
- You make me happy because ...
- I love my dog.
- I love you.
- I smelled the sweetest southern magnolia flower today, and I loved it.

Chanting, Toning Sounds, and Deep Breathing

- Chanting: The word YAM resonates with Heart Chakra. Say YYYAAAMMM as if the sound is coming from your Heart. Follow the same directions used for Root Chakra.
- Say the chant Om Mani Padme Hum. The closest translation is "The jewel is in the lotus." You can find many renditions of it on the internet. Once you learn the words and the rhythm, it can be so much fun to chant. Just let it happen!
- Toning sounds: Tibetan or Himalayan singing bowls. Any instrument that plays the note D resonates with Heart Chakra.
- Take long, slow, deep breaths. Let the breath expand your rib cage, then exhale slowly and feel yourself letting go of all that does not serve you. Inhale to the count of four and exhale to the count of five.
- The element for the Heart Chakra is air. Go outside on a windy day and experience how the air feels, especially when it is charged with excitement. Get creative with how you notice the air. How does it affect the leaves, the clouds, the animals, the water? Imagine it has color and see it swirling around in front of you. Notice how the air perks up your Heart Chakra. You may not want to go back in the house because it feels so good!

The Deconstructed Throat Chakra

Fifth Chakra—Throat Chakra
Sanskrit name: Vishuddha
Meaning: purification
Location: at thyroid
Color: blue
Main focus: tactfully saying what you mean, expressing self without fear of judgment from others.
Gland: thyroid
Developmental age: twenty-eight to thirty-five years
Associated sense: expression and sense of hearing
Element: ether/space
Musical note: A
Supporting stones: sapphire, blue topaz, lapis lazuli, celestite, turquoise, blue calcite
Supporting foods: fruit, especially fruit that grows on vines like berries

Governs: jaw, neck, throat, mouth, tongue, teeth, ears, nose, thyroid, cervical vertebra

Has to do with authentic expression. Purposefully saying what you mean with grace. Saying what you want rather than what the other person wants to hear. Speaking your truth without fear of being rejected. Communicating who you are through words, expression, actions, or creativity.

Physical dysfunctions: sore throats, neck ache, thyroid issues, hearing problems, teeth/gum issues, sinus infections, tight shoulders, TMJ, hoarseness in throat, ear infections

Emotional dysfunctions: perfectionism, feeling disempowered, loud or overly boisterous, no "filter," non-expressive

Archetypes: communicator (functional), masked self (dysfunctional)

When this Chakra is too open, individuals will appear overly talkative, gossipy, dogmatic, arrogant, and self-righteous. They will be poor listeners and extremely loud talkers, dominating the conversation, needing to have the last word, and rambling without a clear point.

When this Chakra is too closed, individuals will appear to be unreliable, inconsistent, quiet, and unheard. They will be deep thinkers who don't let you in. They will not have an opinion and will be unable to defend themselves. They shut down during difficult conversations.

When this Chakra is balanced, individuals will be good communicators and content. They will speak with clarity, listen, and be able to express themselves creatively and confidently share new ideas. Good expression does not always have to be in the form of words. Art, dance, singing, body expression, and career choice are also forms of expressing your truth.

How to Balance Vishudda (Throat Chakra)

Yoga Poses

1. Salamba Sarvangasana—Shoulder Stand Pose (or legs up against the wall)
2. Ustrasana—Camel Pose (hands to back of hips)
3. Halasana—Plow Pose
4. Simhasana—Lion Pose (with vocalization)
5. Matsyasnan—Fish Pose

Meditate

Bring your awareness to the Throat Chakra. Using your mind's eye, visualize the brilliant color blue. As you inhale, use your intention to breathe in blue light, then watch it make its way into your Throat Chakra.

Practice, Think Before You Speak, Listen

Practice what you want to say in front of the mirror until it rolls off your tongue with ease. Then do what Mrs. Roosevelt suggested and do what scares you, which in this case is speaking your truth. Go say what you want to say, with intentions of grace and love. Expressing your true self at first will feel unnatural and scary, but after a few times, it gets easier and easier.

Think before you speak.

1. Is what you're about to say *true?*
2. Is what you're about to say *necessary?*
3. Is what you're about to say intended with *grace?*

YOU'RE NOT YOUR CAR

If you are speaking with highest and best intentions in mind, what you say will always be steeped in grace and Love.

Listen.

Listening to each other is becoming a lost art. How often do you have a conversation with another person, and you know he or she just isn't listening? The highest form of listening is giving the other person your *full* attention, which includes caring about what they have to say as well as turning off electronic devices. Hearing *and* listening to what someone else has to say is a huge component of having a balanced Throat Chakra and can be challenging for someone with an imbalance. With practice, balance, and Love, it can be done!

Read Aloud, Sing Aloud

Making noises and expressing the inner, hidden part of who you are is a fabulous way to get the Throat Chakra activated. Read stories to your children, or your spouse, or your dog, or your plant! Every one of those living beings will absolutely love the energy that comes from your calm voice. Join a singing group and release the energy that may be stagnant in your throat. Turn up the volume and sing in the car. No one will ever know how off-key you are, not even you.

Chanting, Toning Sounds, and Lion's Breath

- Chanting: The word HAM resonates with Throat Chakra. Say HHHAAAMMM as if the sound is coming from your throat. Note: The word Ham is not pronounced like the ham that at one beautiful time in its existence was a pig. It sounds a little bit more like a combination of Ham and Hum. It rhymes with the man's name Tom. Follow the instructions from Root Chakra.

- Toning Sounds: Tibetan or Himalayan singing bowls. Any instrument that plays the note A resonates with Throat Chakra.
- Lion's Breath—take a deep breath, open your mouth wide, stick out your tongue, and say HAAAAAAA!

Be Aware

Just simply bringing awareness to your Throat Chakra will stimulate and nourish it. This is true for *all* Chakras. The awareness of the vortices of energy within your being is the first and very best step to start healing your entire energy system.

The Deconstructed Third Eye Chakra

Sixth Chakra—Third Eye Chakra
Sanskrit name: Ajna
Meaning: To perceive, to know, beyond wisdom
Location: Above and between eyebrows
Color: Indigo
Main focus: To harmoniously fuse intuition and wisdom to be used for greatest potential of knowing. Finding clarity.
Gland: pituitary

Developmental age: can be developed at any age, but for many it's thirty-five years and upward.

Associated sense: seeing/knowing/feeling (sixth sense)

Element: light/telepathic energy

Musical note: E

Supporting stones: amethyst, lapis lazuli, lemurian seed crystal, fluorite, kyanite

Supporting foods: blueberries, foods rich in omega-3, cacao, reishi mushroom, gotu kola (herb), lavender, cannabis plant

Governs: eyes, head, lower part of brain

Has to do with opening your awareness to higher realms. One who successfully uses the Third Eye is no longer focused on balancing lower Chakras because they have already mastered them. Ajna balances intuition and wisdom/intellect. Ultimately the intellect gives way to wisdom. It connects you to a Universal knowing without the influence of your past, or your expectations, or your judgment, or preconceived notions. With a highly evolved Third Eye, you are able to receive information and wisdom without relying on the five senses. Intuition becomes very fluid, allowing the individual to sense beyond the physical realm.

Physical dysfunctions: headaches, neurological disturbances, eye issues, mental fog, insomnia, clogged sinuses

Emotional dysfunctions: nightmares, learning difficulties, hallucinations, depression

Archetypes: psychic (functional), rationalist (dysfunctional)

When this Chakra is too open, individuals will appear to be schizophrenic or living in fantasy. They will have nightmares, be overwhelmed, experience unusual phenomena and be very shaken by it.

When this Chakra is too closed, individuals will appear to be dogmatic, overly rational, highly analytical, scientific, close minded, and arrogant. They do not dream and feel stuck in the day to day. They are unable to look beyond their own opinions and are unable to see the bigger picture.

When this Chakra is balanced, individuals will be charismatic, highly intuitive, lucid dreamers, and non-materialistic. They will experience unusual phenomena but be unshaken by them.

How to Balance Ajna (Third Eye Chakra)

Yoga Poses

1. Balasana—Child's Pose
2. Makarasana—Dolphin Pose (Down Dog on forearms instead of hands)
3. Vrikshasana—Tree Pose (when you are balanced inside, you are balance outside)
4. Prasarita Padottanasana—Wide-legged Forward Fold (brings your perspective to a new position, allowing for greater opportunity for transcendence)
5. Adho Mukha Svanasana—Downward Dog Pose

Meditate

Bring your awareness to your Sixth Chakra. Using your mind's eye, visualize the brilliant color indigo (or any other variation of purple). As you inhale, use your intention to breathe in indigo light, then watch it make its way into your Third Eye.

One of the best ways to open the Third Eye is through meditation. Some people begin to feel a tingling sensation or a light pressure on the forehead between the brows. This is a sign the Third Eye is activating. Having an open mind, being open to all possibilities, and coming from a place of love will also help to activate or balance this Chakra.

Try these mantras as you begin your meditation.

– I recognize the need for stillness in my life.

- Making mistakes enables me to know more.
- I trust in my imagination and my feelings.
- I am my Soul's plan in action.
- The answers to all my questions lie within me.
- I choose to accept myself and all that is, exactly the way it is.
- I can and do create a world of happiness for myself.
- I can manifest a life and fill it with all I desire.

Brahmari (or Bee Breath)

Take a moment to get the correct finger placement. Bring both hands to your face. Place the two middle fingers in the inside corners of your eyes and up against the bridge of your nose. Allow the index fingers to rest on the eyebrow line and place the pinky fingers under the cheekbones. Let your ring fingers just naturally rest on your cheeks. Close your ears with your thumbs. (If this is too cumbersome, just focus on thumb and middle finger placement.) Take a deep breath in. Exhale the word Om with the emphasis on the "M" sound while creating a buzzing/humming sound as if a bee was humming. Let the sound of Om resonate in your sinuses for as long as your breath will allow. Do this for two or more minutes. You can alleviate tension in the head with this technique, as well as open your Third Eye. The fingers placed at these specific points allows you to consciously follow the flow of energy from the pinkies, to the ring fingers, to the middle fingers, to the index fingers, and into the Sixth Chakra. Closing your ears allows you to go within.

Chanting, Toning Sounds, and Candle Gazing

- Chanting: The word Om resonates with Third Eye Chakra. Say OOOOOOMMM as you focus your attention on the Third Eye.

- Toning sounds: Tibetan or Himalayan singing bowls. Any instrument that plays the note E resonates with the Third Eye Chakra.

Meditation for Ajna Chakra (candle gazing)

Step one

Sit in a comfortable meditation posture and take a moment to calm your mind and body. Take a few cleansing breaths to clear your mind. Breathe deeply and slowly to release stress from your mind and tension from your body.

Step two

Now gaze at the flame of the candle. Don't let yourself go into a stare or irritate your eyes. Just gaze at it for as long as you can. Don't worry if your eyes tear up. When you are unable to keep your eyes open any longer, close them and keep them closed.

Step three

Keep your mind still and allow a mental image of the flame to come into your mind's eye. At this point you want to simply observe. Don't force an image. Just let it be, let it form. If nothing manifests, don't worry. Stay calm and try again. Take a couple of deep, relaxing breaths. Now, let the image appear.

Step four

Open your eyes once again and gaze at the flame. Keep your eyes open but keep them calm and relaxed. After a minute or two, close your eyes and keep them closed.

Step five

Just as you did in the previous round, observe your mind's eye, and wait for the candle to manifest. Maybe you will only see the outline of the candle, maybe you will see something like a dark shape, or maybe you won't see anything. Keep observing and give your mind the time it needs to manifest this image on your mental screen. Once again, breathe deeply and cleanse your mind.

Step six

Open your eyes one last time and gaze at the flame for as long as your eyes allow. Then close your eyes and let them relax.

Step seven

Observe your mind's eye as you begin to see the candle flame. The more you do this the easier it gets. Simply observe and don't try to force the image to appear. It has to appear naturally and by itself. Breathe deeply and clear your mind.

Listen to your body as you do this practice. If your eyes become too irritated, stop for a while.

If you are successful finding the image of the candle in your mind's eye, move on to more challenging images. You can look at a tree outside, then try to find it in your mind's eye. Then try a piece of furniture, your sleeping pet, etc.

Once you have mastered this, try thinking very clearly and intently about an object. Don't physically look at it. Just think about it for a few minutes. Keep your mind clear. Try not to have wandering thoughts. Next, close your eyes and try to visualize what you were thinking about. It may not be as clear as the candle flame was. It may be a bit washed out, but you will be able to tell if even a faint image comes in. This practice will help you develop your Third Eye and make meditating easier. Don't worry if you are never successful with this exercise. Having the awareness of something is just as powerful. Remember the exercise we did in the beginning of the book. Have a friend sit with you. Close your eyes. Have your friend slowly call out things to you like a blue truck, a black dog, a puffy white cloud, a red Chakra. You may not actually see these images behind your eyelids like photos on your phone, but if you can bring the essence of these images into your awareness you will be doing something absolutely amazing.

The Deconstructed Crown Chakra

Seventh Chakra—Crown Chakra
Sanskrit name: Sahasrara
Meaning: thousand-fold
Location: top/crown of head
Color: violet, white, sometimes gold
Main focus: spirituality, selflessness, complete transcendence, and enlightenment.
Gland: pineal
Developmental age: any age
Associated Sense: beyond self, silence
Element: thought/celestial energy
Musical Note: B

Supporting stones: selenite, clear quartz, angel hair quartz, diamond, white jade, white tourmaline, celestite

Supporting foods: fasting, inhaling blue lotus flower, ginkgo

Governs: brain, cerebral cortex, skull, skin

Has to do with complete transcendence into the All. It is a Chakra concerned with enlightenment and spiritual connection to all that is. This Chakra offers connection to Source Energy and to every being in the Universe.

Physical dysfunctions: Alzheimer's, epilepsy, exhaustion, sensitivity to large or loud or crowded places, skin disorders

Emotional dysfunctions: confusion, depression, obsessive thinking, fear of death

Archetypes: guru (functional), egocentric (dysfunctional)

When this Chakra is too open, individuals will appear psychotic, manic-depressive, confused, and with a sense of unrealized power.

When this Chakra is too closed, individuals will appear to be constantly exhausted. They will have a sense of not belonging. They can't make decisions, have no connection to a higher power, and are skeptical.

When this Chakra is balanced, individuals will seem to have a magnetic personality. They seem to have miracles at work in their lives. They are transcendent, at peace with themselves, and enjoy quiet and peace in nature while still being able to exude high spirituality in loud, chaotic places.

How to Balance Sahaswara (Crown Chakra)

Yoga Poses

Any pose that brings Crown Chakra toward the floor.

1. Adho Mukha Svanasana—Down Dog
2. Uttanasana—Standing forward bend

3. Salamba Sirsasana—Headstand (use forearms to support neck, can be done with toes on floor)

Meditate

Bring your awareness to the Crown Chakra. Using your mind's eye, visualize the brilliant color white. As you inhale, use your intention to breathe in white light, then watch it make its way into Crown Chakra. Visualize a beautiful white lotus flower of a thousand petals inhabiting the space of your Crown Chakra. See those petals delicately opening into full bloom as white light illuminates each petal, creating an iridescent glow of Love Energy. Now, using your intention, allow this energy to travel through your Chakra system, filling each of the six lower Chakras with beautiful Love Energy. Stay here in this tranquil peace that you have created.

Silence

Silence is one of the most powerful ways to open this Chakra, but we have so few opportunities to experience true silence in our modern world. Silence can even make some people feel uneasy. In silence, you may find your mind wanders, but with practice you will start to stay in silence longer and longer regardless of material or emotional distractions. When you are able to quiet your mind in silence, you will feel a deep relaxation start to come over your body. This practice of being in silence can be very enlightening for the Soul, therapeutic for the body, and relaxing for the mind.

Practice this with the phone turned off and when you are not needed by children, pets, work, spouses, etc.

The Results

Once you've established a daily practice of meditation and feel comfortable in silence, you will begin to connect to Universal Consciousness. You will see an expansion of Universal awareness in your inner and outer world. You will start to understand non-duality. You will be more compassionate, kind, and forgiving, and show more humility. Life will no longer be focused on material objects or what you desire. Instead, you will find great joy in serving others, because when you serve others, you are serving yourself. You will begin to know this because, in understanding non-duality, you will begin to understand there are no individuals. Instead, we are all one. A droplet of water reunited with the sea and living in a *constant* state of pure awareness may seem unsurmountable. (Or maybe it seems like something you don't want to ever achieve.) But as your awareness of all things becomes clearer and clearer, it will feel most natural. For now, just take baby steps. Instead of jumping into the deep end, try living in *moments* of pure awareness. Try it on for size and experience how good it feels.

Crown Chakra Mantras for Your Meditation

- I am now connecting with my higher self.
- I am a unique, radiant, and loving being.
- Limiting thoughts are released.
- White light fills my entire body.
- I choose to live my life from a place of love and contentment.
- I recognize I am a beautiful note in the symphony of the Universe. Without me, the masterpiece would be incomplete and imperfect.

Chanting, Toning Sounds, and Silence

- Chanting: The word Om resonates with Crown Chakra. The written word seems the same for both Sixth and Seventh Chakras, but there is a difference in the pronunciation. For Crown Chakra, there are three sounds. A, U, and M. The A has the same sound as Ah, the sound used for satisfaction. "Ahh, this chair is comfy!" The second sound is Oh, the sound used to acknowledge something. "Oh, okay, I got it!" The last sound is Mmm. "Mmm, this kale is delicious!" So you will chant Crown Chakra Om as AAAAUUUMMM. Focus your attention on the Crown Chakra as you do this.
- Toning Sounds: Tibetan or Himalayan singing bowls. Any instrument that plays the note B resonates with Crown Chakra.
- Enjoy silence

I Found Silence

Finding silence in our modern world is almost impossible. Even as I write these words my email dings, a motorcycle zooms by outside, far off in the distance a lawn mower roars, and even when it's quiet, my heating and air conditioning system hums softly. I'm not bothered by these sounds. They're part of our life, after all, and life is good.

But I did find it once. It wasn't my goal. I wasn't on a quest for it. I just stumbled upon it, and it was amazing. I found divine silence after hiking for three days to the top of a mountain in Alaska, across the valley from Mt. McKinley. It was August, and all the bears were down in the valley fishing for salmon. With my biggest threat stomping in the streams far below me, I felt relaxed and invulnerable. I sat down to rest on a grassy plateau. At this altitude there were no trees, no bushes, and few low-growing plants. I leaned my back up against an inviting rock and let my head fall backward to soak up the sun's rays. After a few minutes, my body settled into stillness, and at that moment I experienced pure silence, an almost indescribable sensation. My world around me became transfixed. My thoughts were very clear. The emotion I was experiencing was flawless peace. Though my body ached from the hike, I felt no pain. Problems waited for me back at home, yet I felt no angst. My momentary taste of silence was not that of basic nothingness. On the contrary, it was a moment of nothing and everything all at once. It was completeness! I could sense the air moving around me, but it wasn't a sense of wind moving across my face, and it wasn't the wind blowing through trees because there were no trees. It was a soft movement of energy that filled the air space. Air that contained within in it a powerful energy field. The muscles in my ears and my eardrums felt like they were resting! There was nothing to hear, yet I could sense the sound of completeness. Or was it the echoes of vibrations of the Universe pulsing its wisdom of wholeness from every direction? Maybe it was the sound of peace from a massive vortex that I and my surroundings were inside of? Whatever it was, this tranquil sound of nothing and everything all at once sounded and felt marvelous, euphoric, enlightening, powerful, gentle, comforting, nurturing, fascinating, peaceful, amazing. I cannot find the perfect adjective for what I experienced! What a gift it would be to humanity if everyone could feel this expansive nothingness filled with everything. How much worldwide peace could it spark?

There is another word that comes to my mind when I remember this silence. Celestial. Celestial silence is a term that seems to stem from Divine Energy. Divine Energy is Love Energy. This silence I experienced—was it Love Energy at its purest? Love Energy is always around us, regardless of the environment or situation we are in. But in my moment, there were no distractions, which allowed Love Energy to appear so obvious to me. In my moment of complete silence, I felt myself in that spot and only that spot with no intrusions, no disturbances. It was the epitome of living in the moment and allowing Love Energy to fill me completely. The most profound part of my experience was just simply the sensation of all problems lifting off me to the degree that joy so easily flooded into my body and into my awareness. Not only was everything alright. It was magical!

That experience happened in 2005. So much life has happened to me and to humanity since then, but my memory of complete silence stays with me as clear as the moment it was unfolding.

FIVE

REAL PEOPLE, REAL CHAKRAS

Many of my clients decide to work with me because they say they need a different approach. They tell me that they have worked with traditional therapists, and while that helped them to a point, they need something more. Something different. They say they need to learn how to see all of life from a different perspective, but they just don't know how to find it. When you start to learn who you are beyond your physical body, you have illuminating moments, allowing many complicated pieces to fall into place. There is a much bigger picture going on that can start to be seen when you begin to change your perspective. When that happens, the experiences that have made you sad, angry, depressed, confused, or defeated will start to have much less control over you. Understanding who you really are can change so much.

Over the years, I've met with many people whose physical ailments are connected to their emotional turmoil. Understanding the nature of Chakras reveals the link between emotion and ailment, empowering you to become more in control of your health. Below are a few examples that show this link. I chose these case studies because they are extreme and clear. The people's names have been changed for privacy, and they have given me permission to tell their story. Keep in mind, we all have a story. It is the nature of being human, and for that reason we should never judge one another.

Rachel: Rachel was beautiful young lady on the brink of a fabulous life, or so it seemed on the surface. She came to me because she was on a journey to gain more spiritual awareness. During this time, she mentioned she was getting frequent rashes on the front of her neck that could not be explained by her dermatologist. The rashes appeared to be hives, so I asked her what she was stressed about. Rachel didn't really have an answer. Life was going great. She was in a fabulous relationship, she had recently graduated from college, and she was starting her dream job. At this point, there did not seem to be an explanation for her severe hives. As we continued to talk, I gently asked her questions that allowed her to start to see herself more clearly. She revealed to me that she had many other physical imbalances surrounding her throat and mouth. At age twelve, Rachel had surgery for a benign thyroid nodule. Following this, she had braces put on her top teeth to straighten out a severe imbalance that had been developing there. Next, at age eighteen, she had reconstructive gum surgery for gums that wore away because of her retainer. At age nineteen, she had her wisdom teeth removed, which resulted in an infection. At age twenty-five, all of her teeth seemed to be in place, but after further conversation she told me she had terrible neck pain, consistent bouts of strep throat, and an eating disorder.

We continued to talk, and soon the last piece of information was revealed. When Rachel was six her parents divorced. She and her younger sister spent equal time with both parents. Her father was passive-aggressive and used guilt as an emotional weapon. She said that even when he was the one in the wrong, he had the ability to make her feel responsible for turmoil within the family. The guilt from him was relentless. She did not feel seen or heard or important in regard to her father. She soon learned to stop speaking her truth, not engage, hold in the rage, and distance herself from that part of the family.

Clearly there was a combination Root and Throat Chakra imbalance going on here, and the eating disorder probably developed years later as a result of an imbalanced Third Chakra and confidence issues. These were the physical results of a Throat Chakra being shut down due to the inability to speak her truth as well as low energy in her Root Chakra because of an unstable family dynamic.

In a situation like this, it's important for the client to become aware of the pain they had endured in the past, especially during developmental years. Often, as adults, we sweep those difficult childhood and adolescent years under the rug. Nurturing the younger version of ourselves is important, as well as being willing to let go of the emotional energy brought on by the experience. As we will discuss, emotions are energy and energy follows thought. When you choose to let go of unwanted energy, it will go, but you must really be ready to choose it. If you're able to do so all at once, that's great. Most of the time it will take supported baby steps, focused intention, and a clear desire to let go of this deeply placed energy. It's often easier to hold on to that which is familiar rather than going down a new and unknown path, even if the familiar is hurting you.

Rachel allowed her buried emotions to ease by understanding that her father was not intentionally trying to hurt her. He was doing what he thought was best, and didn't realize this type of parenting was not supportive to her. Eventually, she learned to take what he had to offer and not be disappointed by what he was not able to give her. Expectations can turn out to be a pitfall. When we have expectations of someone and they are not met, we immediately feel disappointment which can then morph into a slew of other emotions. Rachel began to understand that even though his actions were perceived by her as negative, from his perspective he was coming from a place of love. Rarely does a person say to themselves, "I am going to behave like this because it is the wrong thing to do." People think they are going about things the right way. It is the person on the receiving end who interprets and feels the impact.

Rachel identified the source of her emotional imbalance, then learned to be joyful in what her father had to offer. What he was not able to offer, she found in other healthy relationships. Rachel also learned how to raise her vibrational frequency and change her thought processes. She has impressed me so much. She's an amazing, intelligent young lady with incredible resilience and strength. Rachel was determined to feel better and worked very hard at remodeling her own expectations of her father. She also sees an eating disorder therapist. She's doing fabulous! Her experience continues to evolve, but she has the tools and awareness to flourish. Recognizing that harboring negative energy will distort one's own energy balance is crucial.

Justine: At the time I knew her, Justine was a happy, positive, and confident fifty-year-old woman. After doing research on her own, she knew her Sacral Chakra was blocked or out of balance. As we started talking, she told me about her physical health and previous surgeries. At the age of seventeen, she had back surgery on her lumbar spine due to a broken vertebra that wouldn't heal on its own. About ten years later, the birth of her daughter was complicated and led to an unplanned emergency C-section. One year after that, a miscarriage led to a D&C that resulted in massive bleeding and pain. A few years later, she was told she had a cyst on her ovary. She checked off every box when it came to PMS, and she experienced overall misery during her periods. During and after her third pregnancy, Justine developed kidney stones, an imbalance that plagued her for twenty years. By the time she was in her late forties, Justine had an appendectomy. At fifty she was fully into menopause and was experiencing all the symptoms it had to offer. Her reproductive organs closed up shop, and her Sacral Chakra was crying out for help.

As Justine became more comfortable with me, she revealed more details. When she was just fifteen years old, she was sexually abused with forced intercourse. A few years later, while she was recovering from back surgery in the hospital, she was sexually abused again by a female night nurse. Shockingly, it happened one more time when she was in college. In her words, "It wasn't as bad because it was more like a date rape." I just wanted to hold this poor woman and let her sob until every bit of her pain flooded out. This was all so heavy, but she wasn't ready to sob.

Our Sacral Chakra thrives when it is allowed freedom of creativity and sexuality. Justine's Sacral Chakra was very closed, very frightened, and the energy flow through it was so low it could not support all the organs and structures it governed. Justine's work was to let go. Not to let go of the memory, but to let go of the energy of the emotions. She needed to let go of fear, hate, and feelings of being broken. What happened to her, happened! There's no getting around that. Once she was able to process and release the emotions that were attached to the events, the events became just another life experience—not great experiences, but experiences, nonetheless. Justine had already worked with a sexual abuse coach who really helped her. Through that work, she was able to let much of the anger, fear, and shame leave her mental and emotional body.

Now she wanted to learn how to heal her Chakra and not feel broken anymore. The surgeries and abuses created a major weakness in the Sacral Chakra. Justine learned to support herself with food, water, acupuncture, herbs, talk therapy, visualization, yoga, VAM chanting, positive thinking, relaxation, doing creative things she enjoyed, and being a powerful energy being. (The Deconstructed Chakra section of this book goes into great detail on how to support each Chakra.) After doing the necessary work on herself, Justine is doing much better, and her Sacral Chakra is finding balance again. One thing I'd like to point out is how she amazingly defined the sexual abuse after her awareness of spirituality concepts expanded. She defined it as something that happened to her body, not her Soul. She experienced it as a Soul, but the violation happened to her body. She said when she recognized her body was her car, it was a turning point for her to let go.

Her emotional body absorbed the emotional pain of the abuse. Her physical body absorbed the physical pain of the surgeries and rape. Yet, through it all, her Soul remained a beautiful being of light that expanded because of the experience.

We all must understand that feeling a situation *and* reacting to it with deep emotion is natural and necessary! It's necessary because it's the only way to fully experience the event. But how we process and store those emotions next is most important.

The emotion must be felt, and then it must be left in the past where it belongs. To carry it with us (whether consciously or subconsciously) will cause the most damage.

When you carry it with you on a conscious level and continuously ruminate over it again and again, telling your story to yourself or whomever will listen again and again, only one thing is accomplished. That is to live it over and over with all the pain, fear, doubt, disappointment, anger, and sadness that it comes with. Regardless of where you carry it, if it still provokes emotional pain when you think about it, it will still create imbalance. You will continuously generate the negative and destructive energy that challenges a Chakra and ultimately harm your body. Equally destructive is "stuffing it away" into the subconscious level. Hating yourself, others, and the situation, and then trying so hard to pretend it never happened, will also cause harm. The energy that came from the event will get stuffed away as well, slowly poisoning your Chakra. Terrible things can happen to us, but we must know that regardless of this terrible thing, we are still beautiful Souls. Beautiful humans. We are not damaged, less, insignificant, lost, spoiled, unwanted, or incomplete. We are exactly who we were before the experience, sometimes even better. And because we are powerful energy beings, we can choose to let go, refocus, and expand. (We will get considerably deeper into this concept later.)

When we carry our pain on a subconscious level, much like Rachel and Justine did, figuring out which Chakra is out of balance and how to fix it can be like detective work.

- First, identify an area of the body that seems to be amiss, the area where most health problems occur. If the emotional event is still new, it may not have affected the physical body yet. But it is still important to deal with the emotion before the body suffers physically.
- From there, identify which Chakra supports this area of the body. An understanding of Chakras and the emotions that

resonate with specific Chakras will then make it more clear where the negative emotional energy has impregnated itself into the body and Chakra.

- At that point most people have a kind of epiphany where it suddenly becomes clear to them how, where, and when the emotional imbalance began. It's almost as if by becoming more aware of the imbalance, memories are awakened, and you intuitively start putting the pieces together.

- For example, if you have always had a challenging relationship with your parent(s) and never felt a good connection to your family or home, you will most likely develop a Root Chakra imbalance—unless you are able to change your perspective. Instead of letting parents and the home create emotional distress, you can accept the fact that your parent cannot provide what you desire because of their own emotional turmoil. You can find the missing connection to your mother or father in another person. Maybe a neighbor or teacher will seamlessly fill the empty space in you that is longing for parent energy. Or can you be willing to recognize your parent is imperfect but still good? Remove your feelings of disappointment toward them and wait to see if the relationship takes on a new life. You may be surprised if you remove your expectations. If you have no expectations of someone, it is impossible for them to disappoint you.

- Root Chakra houses the energy or feeling that declares you need a tribe to belong to. Just because you were born into a certain group of people doesn't mean you are required to assign them the title of family. Family is your tribe of people who love you unconditionally and support your ideas. They are the people you can feel comfortable being yourself around, where you can be you and everyone loves you because of that. But you should know that this is not a free pass to disassociate yourself from the family you were born into just because things seem a little rocky. Sometimes the change that is needed must come from you. Being open to new ideas and allowing those you have relationships with to be the person *they* need to be is all a part of finding perfect balance.

- If you can change your emotional reactions to life situations in a positive and healthy manner, Chakras will usually find balance again with very little effort (though the physical body will need nurturing and time to heal if it has become affected). Change the perspective you view your challenges from and maybe your challenges will start to seem a little less daunting.

Debra: It really doesn't matter how old you are, Chakras can find balance again. Your physical body may show signs of a long-life with many battle scars that seem like they will be with you forever, but your energy body can find health again no matter what your age is. The challenge for older people is they sometimes react to life through their limiting beliefs (beliefs that have incorrectly defined their perceived experiences) and through old habits.

I have this health problem because it's in my genes. My mother had this problem, her mother had it, and now I do. I was going to get this disease no matter what.

Another narrative that can take place within the private thoughts of the mind, or outwardly, can sound like this. *I've been doing it like this for years. Change is difficult, and I really can't image handling this situation differently.*

My wonderful client Debra urged me to make sure her case study was included in this book because, in her words, this is what people need to know to fix their Chakras!

Debra is a seventy-seven-year-old woman, and her health is impeccable! She doesn't take any medications, she doesn't suffer from serious health issues, and has a family history of longevity. In spite of this, Debra first came to me with back issues that were debilitating and were causing her poor quality of life. What she wanted to do more than anything was to be able to go for walks with her dog and her friends. After visiting with an orthopedic surgeon, she was contemplating surgery. I advised against it. Surgery could create more health problems for her, and there was no guarantee it would solve the back pain. I highlighted these details for her:

- Anesthesia could challenge her memory capabilities.
- She would have guaranteed muscle atrophy after surgery.
- She would have guaranteed respiratory decline after surgery.
- She would have risk of infection after surgery.
- She would compromise muscles that were already very tight.

Instead, I recommended a weekly deep-tissue massage, a rigorous abdominal strengthening routine, yoga, and old-fashioned stretching. In addition, I taught her how to use a tennis ball to treat trigger points.

Within three weeks she was feeling great! Her pain level was *down* eighty percent.

This is an example of an older person embracing change and doing something different to create what she wanted. For some younger generations, implementing these therapies may not seem like a challenge. But for someone from a generation that is accustomed to taking a pill the doctor told them to take, or submitting to surgery because the doctor said so, these new routines are enormous.

At her last appointment we were going over a few trigger-point details and it appeared she was having a hard time hearing me. Debra wears hearing aids in both ears, and she said her hearing was just getting worse and worse. She seemed upset.

I said, "That's a Throat Chakra problem."

Intrigued, Debra was ready to explore this idea further. After I asked all the right questions, I learned that in addition to losing her hearing, Debra also had dental issues. She was grinding her teeth so badly that they were cracking. Her sense of smell and taste were fading away, and she had a very mild condition of dysphagia (choking on food or saliva). In the past she had a sinus infection that, evidently, took years to clear up.

In addition to this, Debra said she tends to not be able to communicate her thoughts easily when she is talking to men in an authoritative position. She said her mind goes blank, or she thinks of the right thing to say hours or days after the incident.

The last piece of physical information was not about her, but her brother. He was about to have surgery on his cervical vertebrae (which is a Fifth Chakra issue). This was a very important piece of information, because if they both had a Fifth Chakra issue, it was possible their Chakra imbalance came from a relationship with someone they both knew. Also, knowing that Chakra imbalances can sometimes take years to manifest, the relationship they shared may have been with a parent.

When I asked Debra about her relationship with her parents she immediately started with her father and a picture of their relationship began to take shape. From her memory as a child, he was a very "scary person". Not only was he over six feet tall, but his demeanor was also intimidating. In the household, he made it clear children were not to be heard. Debra was never allowed to voice her opinion. She was constantly being told she was a disappointment, and when she tried to speak up for herself, her father quickly shut her down, both verbally and emotionally. She said the feeling she associated with this treatment was being pushed down and gagged. Her bedroom was directly above the kitchen, and when her parents discussed her behavior, she could hear the words coming up through the vent in her floor like daggers hitting her ears. Yet she was voiceless to defend herself. In retrospect, Debra remembers her young self as being a good kid, contrary to how she was treated by her father. "I would get in trouble for not cleaning dust off my bicycle. Another time, I remember running through the house with tears streaming down my face as he chased after me with a leather belt."

As Debra told each story, I could see she still held so much pain, as if she was right back in that moment having the same experiences she had had as a young child and teen. So together we worked out a plan, and this is what we came up with.

1. You hold so much pain from so long ago, so the first thing you have to do is let the emotion out. Tell your stories. Work with a coach, or tell your dog, or tell your Guardian Angel, or tell the wind. Write everything down on a piece of paper. Get it out of you, and as you do, let the emotion out as well. Another idea is to visualize your father sitting with you (in this instance, Debra's father had already crossed) and tell him exactly how he made you feel, how he wronged you, and that your opinions matter! Get clear on how you want to speak aloud that which you have never been able to speak before.

2. If you have written your story down on paper, create a ritual for letting it go. For some, that means burning the paper to represent closure. If you spoke into the wind, visualize the wind taking your emotions away. Speaking to a friend or even a pet can feel cathartic when a loved one bears witness to your hardship. If you visualized speaking directly to your father, imagine how he—a more empathetic and enlightened being now that he has crossed—would hear you the way you always wanted to be heard.

3. After the emotions have left, take a few days or however long you need to feel a healing come over you. If you feel you need to go through each exercise a second time, do it. After you have emptied all your emotions, you will start to think about these memories from a stronger perspective. When it is obvious to you that you are now operating form a stronger place, revisit the events once again, but just be a fly on the wall. Observe what is happening. Notice how, as a girl, you reacted to these unfortunate events in a way

that was very fitting for a young child or teenager. But now you are a strong, capable, independent woman who has the power to respond appropriately, regardless of a person's gender, age, size, demeanor, or aggression. Do this while always remembering balance! You can respond and be heard but do it with grace, kindness, confidence, and from a place of love. As you watch each episode in your mind, recognize how they formed you and created the person you became. With this new knowledge, try to reinvent yourself. Know that you don't have to continuously react to or be controlled by your experience. And know you are in control. At any moment you need to stop this exercise, just stop! Begin again when the time is right.

4. The last piece is forgiveness. Your father conducted himself the best way he knew how. He was a product of his own parents. He may have had many shortcomings and he may have had very poor parenting skills, but he was probably replicating what he witnessed as a child. Just like everyone else, he has a story. He came from somewhere. This does not excuse his behavior toward you, but it does give you an insight as to where his actions came from. What Chakras were out of balance for him? What hardships did he face as a child, as an adult, as a husband, as an employee, as a human? Once you truly forgive, and empty the anger, sadness, and fear out of your Chakra, you will start to realign balance in your energy system and regain balance in your physical body.

As an older person, it is important to balance your Chakras, but some may not be convinced at first.

"What's the point?"

"I'm older now. I have nothing left to learn."

"What's done is done. I'm just going to coast for my next ten to twenty years."

If you don't understand who you are and what your goals are in this particular lifetime, you will very likely be redoing a similar version of it again in your next life. Your Soul wanted you to have the full experience, after all. Not just part of it.

Ted: I absolutely adored Ted. He was about sixty-eight years old when we last worked together, and he had the biggest heart I ever met. He was soft spoken. Very polite. He was the kind of person who didn't say much in a crowd, but when he did, everyone stopped to hear what he had to say. His words were golden pieces of wisdom. But Ted had early-onset Alzheimer's. I created a safe place for him to talk, and when his memory didn't serve him, I would email his family members for key pieces of information. Here's Ted's story.

Ted was the second-born son of Italian and Irish parents. He also had a much younger sister. As the second-born son, he was less doted on than his older brother. Whether this was customary behavior with all Italian mothers at that time, or unique to his family, I cannot say. Regardless, Ted said at times he felt unimportant. From a Chakra perspective, this meant he did not fully develop his sense of self (Sacral Chakra) and did not feel heard (Throat Chakra). He attended parochial school, and years later it was revealed that Ted was a victim of the Catholic Church sexual abuse scandal. From this event(s), his Root Chakra suffered because of fear. His Root Chakra was further compromised because the priests and sisters beat the boys when they did anything they considered out of line. Ted's Sacral Chakra was also certainly compromised from the sexual abuse. His Solar Plexus Chakra became imbalanced due to lack of control. His Throat Chakra continued to suffer because he felt he could not speak up. His parents were devout Catholics and would not tolerate talk against the priests. Besides that, during those times, taking the side of a child over a person of authority just wasn't done. I'm sure there were a number of other reasons he felt he could not speak up.

The Root and Crown Chakras are polarizing energy as they are the grounding force to the earth and the connection to Source energy. As you remember, Source energy is the same energy that many refer to as God. These priests were intimately connected to God, and so Ted's confusion around God, safety, and fear became unmanageable, creating so much damage to the Root and Crown Chakras. Amazingly, it seemed Ted's Heart Chakra thrived despite all this. He had so much love to give, and he saw beauty in everything. Unfortunately, years of privately dealing with this pain and confusion eventually manifested itself into Alzheimer's disease, as well as lower lumbar spinal stenosis. He also suffered other physical imbalances from his Sacral Chakra. About eight years after Alzheimer's had become apparent, Ted left his physical body. With a smile on his face, he grabbed his hat, got up out of his driver's seat and shut the door. He looked fabulous as he walked away from that car of his.

Think About This

Try to determine which Chakras may be out of balance for you.

1. What parts of your physical body seem to be out of balance most often? (Which body parts hurt or have disease?)

2. Can you think of an emotional challenge you've had that seems to reoccur in your life?

3. Is there one really big experience you have had that you perceived as negative and can't let go of?

4. Was there a specific difficult event in your life that seemed to be a turning point for you? Was there more than one difficult event?

5. Do you revisit these events in your mind or talk about them often with people you know (do you keep the emotional energy alive concerning these events in an unhealthy way)?

6. Have you stuffed these feelings away because it's hard to talk about them?

7. Are you able to leave these emotions in the past where they happened and see yourself as a beautiful, powerful, creative being that is so much more than a physical body?

8. Do you feel supported?

9. Do you feel safe?

10. List out your personality traits. Which Chakras do they connect to?

11. Do you feel your personality traits show you are balanced or imbalanced in your Chakras?

12. Which Chakra balancing activities listed in the Deconstructed Chakra chapter do you already do on a regular basis? Which would you like to start doing?

13. Can you make these balancing activities a routine in your life?

14. What's your favorite color? Least favorite color?

15. If you had the power to change a situation in your life, what would you change?

16. Why do you think you don't have the power to change it?

17. What changes would you like to see in yourself?

18. What's stopping you from making those changes?

SIX

THE UEF, OUR ONE-STOP SHOP

The Universal Energy Field

Think back to grade school when you were first learning about planets, the galaxy, stars, and the amazing Universe. Do you remember the mnemonic "My Very Educated Mother Just Served Us Nine Pizzas"? That one is a little dated now, ever since Pluto was downgraded to a "dwarf planet" in 2006. So, what's the updated mnemonic? I think mom is just serving noodles now. She's tired of cooking nine pizzas!

When I was in grade school and the teacher explained the Universe, I pictured a vast, empty, dark place filled with stars, planets, and meteors. Now, read that again. Empty and filled. My goodness, that's an oxymoron! Regardless, my young mind still thought of the Universe in that way. And I thought it was far, far away. It's difficult to fathom the concept of the Universe, for children *and* adults!

To understand the Universe in very basic terms of spirituality, we need to find a good analogy here, and finding a very good one is going to be tough because the Universe itself is immense. It contains everything. It has within it the energy needed to create anything. The Universe is aware of your wants and desires and can reflect them back to you.

At the risk of degrading the integrity of the Universe by using this good but subpar parallel, let's quietly tiptoe over to this analogy: The Universe is like Google (assuming everything you read on Google is accurate).

Within Google you can find the answers to anything! If you want it, it's probably out there on Google. If you're wondering about something, Google probably knows. If you want to create something, Google can help get the materials, ingredients, supplies to help you build it. If you need answers, Google's got it. At all times, you can be directly connected to this massively extensive bank of information that just keeps on giving.

If you don't know something exists, however, Google will not send you that information. You have to be ready to know about it first. You have to formulate the question and type it into the search bar. This means, what you want must first be in your awareness. If you don't want to know something, or don't know it's something that can be known, Google won't send it into your brain or make it flash across your screen in bright red letters. For example, here are a few things other people wanted to know, but you, at this point, have no desire to know. Therefore, they are not on your radar. They are not in your awareness.

"Is there a spell to become a mermaid that actually works?"

"What do I do if a dolphin wants to mate with me?"

"Germany is in what country?"

"Why is my face on my head?"

(I'm serious. People have asked these questions. They're in a list of the twenty most weird searches on Google.) Have you ever wanted to know answers to these questions? I'm going to bet most of these searches, if not all, never seemed important to you. Whether it's because you didn't know being a mermaid was a choice, or you didn't know a spell was required to make it happen, the idea never came into your awareness. Maybe you don't swim in the ocean, so a dolphin sexually having her way with you is not your concern. These are questions and topics you have no interest in, so not only do you not care to ask about them, but you also have no idea that the answers are out there on amazing Google to enlighten you.

When Google becomes aware you *are* interested in something, the information about that thing starts to pop up without you even asking for it.

Now imagine you are inside of Google. You are inside the place where everything is. All you could ever need or want is right before you. All the energy of what is and what can be is swirling around you. The materials for you to create or have anything you want is within your reach. You just have to focus on it and then type it in the search bar.

What if you wanted a pizza delivered to your house? You would type into the search bar "pizza delivery near me." From there you let Google bring you what you need, and you continue to put into motion the steps necessary to get a pizza to your front door. Easy-peasy! But if you typed into the search bar "I'll never get pizza delivered to me," Google will not, cannot, shall not participate in getting a pizza delivered to you.

This is precisely how the Universe works! Well, not precisely. I certainly don't want to make it seem like Google is as amazing as the Universe. This is just an analogy, but it's another good analogy to help you break down those walls on which you have spray-painted, *This is way too complicated for me to ever understand.* Now you can start to understand the power the Universe with more clarity, right?

Like everything on earth and in Spirit, the Universe is made up of energy. That vast, empty space is not only filled with planets and stars, it's also filled with energy. This energy is vibrating in the black space that we see when we look up at night. It's the endless region of infinity that holds countless galaxies, black holes, worm holes, and all the powerful momentum necessary to create anything we want. It also weaves through the proximity of space directly around us as we exist here on earth. Yep, that's right! The Universe and its energy are right here, right next to you. As we discussed earlier, this energy is known as Universal Energy, or the Universal Energy Field (UEF).

Scientists are able to measure it, and some scientists refer to it as bio-plasma. As more and more of humanity starts to become reawakened to life beyond physicality, we are seeing that science is taking a keen interest in centuries-old foundational concepts, like alternative healing, energy healing, meditation, and manifestation.

In the book *Mind to Matter* by Dawson Church, science takes a very close look at these ancient concepts. Though the book is steeped in scientific vernacular, it is clear the scientists are very impressed with their findings as they discuss the fabulous results of carefully conducted experiments. These scholars are reporting that meditation can heal the body. Manifestation is real. Energy healing can reverse cancer cells *from a remote location!* We are starting to see modern science taking steps away from the safety of the mainstream and proving things that were once considered a little too woo-woo to even be considered. And they are also talking about the UEF.

While many of us don't need science to validate that we are powerful energy beings, and that meditation and energy can heal, it's nice to see those who once denounced its usefulness and abilities are finally in step with the pervasive wisdom of centuries.

So, back to the UEF. Because it's like a bio-plasma, it permeates all space and connects all objects to each other. The plasma of our own body is a connective tissue that carries all necessary nutrients and hormones to all parts of the body. Similarly, the UEF contains within it all the information needed for enlightenment as we Souls live our human experience. Cells put their waste products into plasma, and we release our negative emotions into the UEF (partly by way of the Earth Star Chakra previously mentioned). Upon release of the negative emotions, the UEF takes this unwanted energy back to the depths of the Universe where it is recycled into more usable energy. Energy cannot be destroyed, only changed.

The UEF is an energy in and of itself and carries within it an innate intelligence that is available to all of us. Now here's the interesting thing about this intelligence we have access to: It is absorbed into us via the Chakras, but we are only able to absorb (or be aware of) the information that we are ready for. If you have not yet reached a higher emotional enlightenment, your Chakras will not absorb frequencies within the UEF that are not yet within your understanding. For example, you wouldn't explain to a small child how to build a skyscraper. The child simply would not understand.

First let the child digest the concept of Legos, then as a teenager he can help his father build a barn, then as a young adult he will build his own house. Slowly, he has gained the knowledge and wisdom of how to build a skyscraper.

Google was one analogy. Another comparison is reading the encyclopedia and coming across words that are completely beyond your comprehension. What would you normally do if this happened? Here are some possibilities:

1. You just skim past the word as if it wasn't even there.
2. You look at the word, try to figure it out, but then realize you just have no idea what it means and then quickly lose interest.
3. You ask for help or research it enough to have a basic understanding, and then stick it in your back pocket until you have an experience that put that word back in front of you. Although you still can't use it in a sentence, you do have more clarity than before. Now the word is on your radar, and next time it comes up, you may even try to fit it into a sentence.

As you grow intellectually, unknown words start to have meaning for you until finally you can wield these words like a scholarly poet. The same is true regarding UEF. As you begin to become more and more enlightened, whether through meditation or experiences or both, you will start to become aware of ideas that are not obvious to those who do not share your path of transcendence (even though these ideas are ultimately available to everyone).

Meet Jane and Amanda

Jane is full of love and welcoming to everyone she meets. There is no room in her life for racism or prejudice. Jane easily makes friends with everyone she encounters because every person is beautiful and equal in her eyes. Anyone who meets her immediately feels a welcoming, accepting love emanating from her. She is delightful and only sees good in people. Though Jane is full of love in this way, she has no compassion for animals or the earth. She doesn't recycle, and she litters! None of her heart strings are tugged when she sees an ASPCA TV commercial for abused or neglected animals. She could simply care less about those dirty creatures.

Amanda, on the other hand, does not think the earth is just a dead thing. She believes that every rock, and tree, and creature has life, and a soul. She belongs to many organizations that save animals, and she adopted three homeless cats and four homeless dogs from her local shelter. She also participates in community trash cleanups and donates a lot of money to foundations that help the earth. Though Amanda is quite passionate about nature, animals, and opening her heart to helpless creatures, she was raised in a racist community and, because of limiting beliefs, does not see all humans as equals. She has been known to use racial slurs for many different groups, and she speaks out against inter-racial marriages.

These two women clearly have good in their hearts, but also have significant spiritual ladders to climb. Where Jane is evolved, Amanda is not. And in the areas Jane needs to let in more awareness, Amanda has already mastered it. Jane can let in the higher concepts of equality from the UEF because she is already open to basic ideas of equality. But she is probably not even aware of the vibrational frequency available to her concerning the environment and animals because it's something that has never really touched her spiritual radar yet. The same goes for Amanda, just flip-flopped. The more they are exposed to new concepts of racism, animal cruelty, climate change, and prejudice, the more opportunities they will have to become aware of the spiritual growth that is available to them. It is very possible for these women to evolve spiritually and someday be sensitive to both situations equally. The more aware they become and the more they exercise their spiritual muscles, the quicker they will evolve to a new way of thinking. Of course, it is also possible they will never become enlightened in this lifetime. But the more they are exposed to a different way, the more likely they will begin to open to new ideas. That is why it takes so long for moral, ethical, and spiritual change to occur within humanity. Racism, cruelty to animals, pollution, inequality ... these are all things that took many years for most people to realize were spiritually wrong, even though the frequency of the knowledge and frequency of that way of thinking has always been available to all of us through all times by way of the UEF. And there are infinitely more frequencies available to us. Not just the ones mentioned here. Accessing them is just a matter of letting the vibrational frequencies into our awareness by being curious and open minded and by simply acting and being loving toward all.

Perhaps one day the collective consciousness of humanity will evolve to an exceptionally high level of spiritual Love. In that moment we will see people as just people, not men or women. Not black or white. Not Christian or Muslim. Just simply as people.

Maybe someday we will all scoff at the idea of eating the flesh of another living creature.

Maybe emotionally violent acts will be considered just as heinous as physically violent acts.

Maybe the idea of working so hard will fall away and enjoying the beauty life has to offer will become more important. Could that be what the younger generations are starting to become aware of in the UEF? Does life really have to be so hard? Millennials who are accused of not wanting to work hard but still expect the luxuries of life may be the pioneers of a new way. They may be the first generation to tap into never-before-used information from the UEF. Information that shows us how to be successful while being carefree. What an amazing thought! What else could the UEF hold within it that we are, at this time, completely unaware of?

(You should also note that Amanda and Jane are fictitious examples created to explain a concept. Don't hate them! You're working on the flow of positive energy, remember?)

Try This

It's very easy to see the UEF even if you have not yet developed your clairvoyance.

Go outside on a very sunny day when the sky is blue. It's okay if you have eyeglasses on, but don't wear sunglasses. While looking up at the sky (*not* the sun) try to let your gaze be very relaxed, almost like you're trying to stare into and beyond the blue sky. Now, without changing your focus, concentrate on the space before the sky. After a few seconds you should start to see bright, sparkling, glitter-like energy, even in the trees and bushes, although it's easiest to see in the sky. If you pay attention to individual pieces of glitter you can see them zooming about in a sort of haphazard direction. While this is not the entire bio-plasma, it's certainly a part of it.

SEVEN

SOUL GOALS AND THEORIES

Why Are We Here?

What's our purpose? These two questions may be the most pondered questions within the private recesses of our minds ever since the beginning of meaningful thought. If existing in Spirit as a Soul is such a blissful experience (as reported by those who have had near-death experiences), why bother getting into this slow vibrating, uncomfortable, limiting body? And why endure physical, emotional, or mental agony during our time in physicality? While it's true we as humans have many beautiful, happy moments on earth, is it worth the amount of suffering that can sometimes go along with it?

Before we get into the depths of that philosophical topic, let's visit some very westernized ideas about why we are here on this planet. These theories, some of which you are probably already familiar with, are not concepts I support. I'm just throwing these out there for you to consider. Maybe you can think of others. At the end, I will offer another, less considered yet sound reason we are here.

The Classroom Theory

This earth, our life, and the events that take place during our human existence is a classroom. It's a place we have incarnated into without much help or direction. The goal is to learn as much about moral and ethical behavior as possible. To do that, we may have to climb out of deep holes after hitting rock bottom, suffering through loss, and weathering many storms. These unfortunate experiences can be a result of our bad decisions, or just pure bad luck. Good times are possible, but they too are provided purely for the benefit of the classroom. If you're lucky, you will learn from your mistakes and suffering, move on, and with more luck find a little utopia before you shed your physical body. At the very end of your life, graduation day, you may be able to look back at your time in the classroom and think, *I wish I had done it all differently. I shouldn't have worried so much. I should have been more joyful. I wish I loved more.* Or maybe you *don't* have these revelations, in which case you will have to repeat that grade again. That is, if you believe in reincarnation. If you don't, then you have just failed at your one and only mediocre life.

The Eye-for-an-Eye Theory

Karma comes from Hinduism, Buddhism, and other Eastern religions. The word karma roughly translates to "action". In theory, it means the actions individuals take will come back to affect them someday in their future. Each religion has slightly different facets regarding karma, and the ideology of karma is quite profound with much deeper meaning than stated here. Our westernized version of karma is rather simplistic. Basically, here in the West, karma is the need to experience the same misfortune we have inflicted upon another from a previous lifetime or earlier in this lifetime. Examples of this premise are as follows.

- If you were a rapist in a previous life, you are destined to be raped in this life.
- If you cheated someone out of their fortune in a previous life, you will lose all your money in this life.
- If you were a cranky, bitter, uncaring, selfish pessimist, then you will marry a cranky, bitter, uncaring, selfish pessimist.

It is the "you get what you give" philosophy.

The Hell-on-Earth Theory

Living a physical existence can undoubtedly be a challenge at times, and if your mantra is "the glass is half empty," earth can easily feel like hell. Nothing ever goes right. There's war, famine, pandemics, cruelty, fires. The climate is creating environmental chaos. Since the beginning of time, evil has been unfolding on the earth. Love is not here. Wherever we were before earth must have been exponentially better than here, but sadly, unscrupulous ways landed us in this hellhole called earth. Others don't see earth as being quite that bad, just half as bad. They refer to our time on earth as purgatory.

This particular theory on why we are here on earth bothers me so much, I feel I must interject a different, better perspective. In fact, I am going to denounce the whole theory!

So, what about all the good things happening on this planet? They may be harder to find because they're not being broadcast by the media as loudly as the bad things are. But they are here! There are medical breakthroughs for those who are suffering, child prodigies are doing mind-boggling things, music and art are being created, couples are falling in love, ideas are being shared, and humanity is starting to turn the page and awaken to the bigger picture. We must keep our eye on the prize, so to speak. And that prize is love and beauty. Love and beauty! It's everywhere! It's in the wind before a rainstorm, it's the feeling of warm sun rays on a cool day, and it's in each unique snow crystal. It's the joy of watching a kid learn to ride a bike or a puppy's first encounter with a butterfly. It's the taste of your favorite food, the feeling of accomplishment, and the peace of just simply sleeping in. It's that new car smell, the feeling of sand between your toes, and crashing out on the couch with dinner to watch your favorite TV show. It's finding a twenty dollar bill on an empty beach, stopping so a goose family can safely cross the road, and coming around a turn to find an unexpected, amazing sunset. It's meeting a new friend and reconnecting with an old one. It's watching a child open presents and the good feeling you get when you help someone in need. It's that weirdly amazing smell of a newborn's head and saying hello again after being away too long. It's finally realizing we are all connected, knowing we can create anything we want, and wanting to create more beauty. Love Energy is still happening all around us constantly, in spite of the doom and gloom that's been going on for so long. It's easy to focus on the surplus of negative information being pumped out at us. But I will wager that if you are reading this book, you're not accustomed to doing what is easy and mainstream. You're hanging out with cutting-edge thought processes that propel you further, bigger, higher! You're not in it for the superficial, cathartic lamestream. And for someone like you, it's easy to focus on joy, peace, and love. In no way does this mean you should bury your head in the sand when adversity creeps in. We have to face the bear when the bear appears! But if right here, right now, in this moment, in this space you are currently existing everything is okay, then let joy, peace, and love shine.

That was flowery, but it had to be said!

The Big-Bang Theory

Last, there is the belief that we humans exist because of a single, infinite hot and dense point that expanded and stretched for billions of years and is still stretching. Then a random biological mishap created life on earth. Thanks to all that, here we are, flourishing on our planet until our bodies expire. Upon expiration, there is no Soul to move on. Our bodies simply cease to exist, our consciousness ceases to be aware, and the impact we leave behind lasts only as long as someone remembers us. Our essence vaporizes into nothingness.

- Do any of these hypotheses ring true for you?
- Do any resonate with your core beliefs?
- Do any of these possibilities make you happy?

As a Soul inhabiting a human body, I don't think any of us emphatically know why or how we are here. That information was lost from our consciousness shortly after we incarnated and that annoying veil came into play.

- We can, if we wish, accept the answers our parents or religious leaders offer. If those answers fit nicely into who you are, then that is wonderful!
- We can just impassively say "who knows!" and go about our lives haphazardly, struggling until the end.
- Or we can meditate, search our Souls, and open our minds to a bigger picture in hopes that an acceptable answer flows to us on the currents of energy. And when it does, this information will make navigating life as a physical being more meaningful and satisfying ... bringing further clarity to who we are beyond our physical body.

So, what do *you* think? What do *you* believe?

You must be aware of the possibilities, consider them, and then land on the one that resonates best with you.

In the end, everyone must come to their own conclusion and be content with the answer that sits best with them.

How does an idea feel when you consider subscribing to it, living by it? Could you explain it to others and feel very confident that you are passing on a good, solid opinion?

After reading, researching, meditating, being involved in discussion groups, talking to like-minded individuals, and connecting with my own spiritual team of Guides, Angels, and higher beings, I finally let all the information I gathered settle and marinate in my being. Some of it resonated with me. I felt good when I considered it. There were also ideas that, when I considered them, did not feel good, so I eventually let them filter out. I allowed my consciousness to stretch to places it had not traveled before. Could I find a space in my belief system for some new ideas? Yes, I thought I could, so I let them in. And then I sat quietly and tuned in to my intuition. The information that flowed to me on those currents of energy from the UEF sounded wonderful. It sounded like this.

First and foremost, we are powerful energy beings. Like the drop of water from the sea, we are a small part of the greatest Creator of all, Source Energy, so of course we also have the inherit power to create. When we are Souls without a physical body, we exist in the realm of Spirit (a.k.a. heaven). In that realm we can easily create whatever we want, go wherever we want, be whatever we want. It takes only the desire and the thought to create it. As Souls, or energy beings, we are very aware of our creative ability. It is our spiritual nature and comes to us as naturally as laughter comes to a human. The possibilities are endless because in the realm of Spirit our vibrational frequencies are so acutely high.

Here on earth, in this physicality, the vibrational frequencies are much slower, making everything around us so much more dense. To experience the possibilities and involvement that only physicality can offer, we must slow our own vibrations considerably in order to interact with the density of a tree, flower, bug, sunset, other humans, our pets, triumphs, delights, passion, sadness, despair, sounds, touch, smells, sights, tastes, sexual intimacy, human inventions, a sense of individuality, and every single emotion.

When we permanently take residence in a body at birth, we slow down our vibration. After a few years of being accustomed to the physical plane, we start to lose our awareness of Spirit (unless a caregiver continues to nurture that part of ourselves, or we chose to retain some of that wisdom before incarnating). As we get older, some of us are vaguely aware of Spirit by way of intuition, or books that resonate with our sensibilities. We have a sort of reawakening. In this state of awareness, the realms of the physical and spiritual seem to be separated by the metaphorical veil. Being aware of this veil motivates us to gently push further into reuniting with that which lies beyond the veil, which is Spirit. Understanding a human existence from the vantage point of Spirit reveals to us that we can enjoy all that being a human has to offer while not completely forgetting the peace and serenity that accompanies the realm of Spirit. By meditating, practicing yoga, raising our vibrational frequency, and harnessing our powerful creative energy, we can still be a part of Spirit while living a beautiful existence on earth. Raising your vibrational frequency is very important to this entire concept.

So, what about that question we started all this with? Why are we here and what's our purpose?

The reason we are here is to *experience* and our purpose is to *create!*

To experience all the emotions and feelings that can only be realized on a physical plane.

To create beauty and more expressions of Love Energy.

And also to know the brilliant perspective of Source Energy from all interpretations of awareness. There's a little bit more to it than that, and we will first need to lay out a little more groundwork before we add more depth to the Soul purpose of experiencing and creating.

But that is our greatest intention … to experience and create what we can not in Spirit. To find the awareness and understanding that Source energy already has. To become as close to Source as possible. In order to do that, we must acquire a greater understanding of ourselves and all that the mysteriously marvelous Universe has to offer.

Before we move on, let's just touch on a very valid point made from the Classroom Theory.

> *"I shouldn't have worried so much. I should have been more joyful. I wish I loved more." Or maybe you don't have these revelations, in which case you will have to repeat that grade again.*

This valid point comes from a less-than-perfect theory, but standing alone, it deserves some attention.

Yes, we are here to create and experience, but while doing so we need to be joyful. Love more! Worry less! More than likely these are parts of the plan you came with. The plan was definitely more complex than just that, but certainly being joyful, loving more, and worrying less were definitely a presumptive part of the plan. Hardships do happen and may even be designed by you (Soul) to happen. But rising up and seizing good feelings in spite of difficulty is transcendence in motion.

Take inventory of yourself and your life right now. Are you completely content and happy? If your answer is no, do you plan to be happy in about five to ten years from now? Yes, of course you do! So, if you plan to be happy in five to ten years, why not just be happy now? Why wait? Do what you need to do now to be happy now. Just look at the good stuff. Stop hyper focusing on the depressing, low-vibrating things. If you can make changes that lead to happiness, do it! If you can't, find new avenues that lead to joy. If you want it bad enough, make it happen. The *you* of five years from now will certainly thank you.

EIGHT

LIMITS, KARMA, AND HELL

Your Limits are Set By You

> *Limiting Beliefs:* Imperfect foundational concepts
> that we have acquired from our parents, family,
> ancestors, teachers, political and religious leaders,
> and even past lives. *These concepts have not been*
> *questioned by us as individuals and eventually turn into*
> *beliefs. They are something we just simply incorporate*
> *into our energy field and our way of thinking when*
> *we are children, and as we mature, we are unaware*
> *of how these beliefs hold us back from success and*
> *happiness. Recognizing these beliefs and releasing them*
> *from our consciousness can be a lifelong journey or can*
> *happen immediately. It is in our control. Limiting*
> *beliefs also halt our ability to create.*

We have all heard of limiting beliefs, but do you realize how
powerful they are at changing the life your Soul intended? These
types of beliefs interrupt the possibility of becoming aware of new
energy thoughts from within the UEF. Limiting beliefs usually come
from individuals or groups that have a profoundly formative effect
on us. This is unfortunate, because we are taking on the thought
patterns and moral standards of those who came before us, people
who did not have the benefit of practicing expanded thinking or
moving through their life with absolute clarity. To our detriment,
we consciously (or subconsciously) assimilate into our being what is
reflected back to us from these sources. Ideas such as "life is hard,"
"we are not all equal," "my religion is better than yours," "I am not

lovable.", fear of rejection, fear of failure, and so many other self-defeating thoughts start to become beliefs that we don't question, and we are usually not aware that they are implanting themselves into some part of our awareness. The ability to create works in both directions. You can create wonderful things for yourself, and you can equally create hardship, misery, and loss. By succumbing to limiting beliefs, we unintentionally start creating a difficult life from the very beginning of our physical lives (or whenever the limiting belief became fixed into our energy system). Limiting beliefs are thoughts, and thoughts are energy. When we focus on a specific thought, the Universe connects us with similar concepts of energy. This is the Law of Attraction at work again. There are so many different types of limiting beliefs, and we all subscribe to some of them, often unintentionally. This is unfortunate because each one will negatively affect one or more Chakras. It's amazing when you start to realize that the way you think about a topic or idea can really hold you back from achieving your goals, or even eventually cause decline in the physical body. Here are just a few very common limiting beliefs that will make your life more difficult. If you believe in these, you will start to create it in your life. Remember, these beliefs can reside in your consciousness as well as your subconsciousness. You are a powerful energy being. If you focus on something long enough, you will create it into physicality.

- I'm not good enough.
- I must work hard to have money.
- There is no justice.
- Life is not meant to be fun.
- I'm too fat.
- I'm too old.
- Life is hard.
- Life isn't fair.
- I was born poor; I will stay poor.
- I'm not smart enough.
- I'm a worrier.
- I am superior to everyone else.
- I am inferior to everyone else.
- I am powerless.
- I'll never find a husband (wife).

- I never get a break.
- Things don't work out for me.
- I'll always be alone.
- _____ disease runs in my family.
- I can never get it right.
- My life is miserable.
- Money is hard to come by.
- If I don't _____ no one will like me.

- I'm always sick.
- Money is something other people have.
- I always lose.
- Happiness is always just out of my reach.
- _____ people are inferior to me.
- _____ people are less important.

They are called limiting beliefs because they limit you from all the endless, wonderful possibilities that are available to you. And they limit you from enjoying the amazing gifts that every single person on the planet has to offer. Later when we discuss the power of creating and how you can easily have anything you want just by putting your attention, intention, and energy forward you will also learn you can create things you *don't* want when you focus on them. Creating is not reserved for just the good things out there. If you continuously put forward the energy that you are always sick, *you will always be sick.* But more on that later.

So, suffering can happen as a result of limiting beliefs, but we are not meant to suffer. The original intention of our Souls is that while we are experiencing, we also have a wonderful, beautiful existence during our incarnation in this world. Love, create, explore, experience! The earth is our playing field for all of this. While it's true some experiences are more challenging than others, it is by our own choice to feel the weight of those challenges for longer than is necessary. Letting go of the emotional pain is key.

Source is All Love and all good. It is counter-intuitive to imagine that a being with only goodness and Love as its foundation would prefer us to incarnate with the intent to suffer. This type of god is in line with one that wants us to be fearful of him, which is such an outdated and controlling way to view god figures. If you love your child, or pet, or self unconditionally, would you want to see them suffer while figuring out how to be happy? You would not if you're coming from a place of unconditional and absolute Love.

Limiting beliefs can not only affect our own lives, but they can also ruin other lives. For example, when a group of people all subscribe to the same limiting belief that they are superior to others, many lives and experiences will be affected. This type of limiting belief not only causes the believer to have stunted spiritual development, reduced life experiences, and a dark emptiness within their being, but the focused target of that limiting belief is now stripped of their *Soul* right to free will. Notice the term "Soul right." In many ways, this is even greater than a "human right." Souls are granted free will from Source. Free will means you have the freedom to choose as you see fit for yourself, as long as you don't harm or limit others.

Let's use the little car example again. Imagine you're driving down the highway and you want to get off the next exit. You're getting ready to take that exit to the right, but out of nowhere, another car purposely comes and smashes into your right side, completely derailing you from your choice to get off the highway! Now your car is not only damaged, but you also have no idea where to go from here. Other exits will take you further from your destination or not get you there at all. This has really upset you. No other car should have the power to intercept you like that, because no other car knows where you came from, where you are going, and what reasons you had to make that turn. Not to mention that it's just plain wrong to violate another car in such a way, and it's against the law! Your freedom to drive on the public highway has just been altered. Your free will is gone.

Source sends you off to have experiences here on earth with free will. And the choices you choose to make, good or bad, are yours to make. No person or group is allowed to tamper with that, yet it happens often. Free will is a law put into effect by a power much greater than any person or group living on this planet.

It is important to distinguish between free will and negative intentions. Free will is meant to allow you the ability to navigate through your life in a way that you feel will best serve you, regardless if it is a part of your Soul plan or not. Negative intentions are harmful to the delicate balance of the Universe and can be directly malicious or destructive toward others. Trying to decide what is a negative intention and what is acting out of free will can be be quite complicated at times. Abortion is a perfect example of this. A baby being born can certainly impact a woman's life and so, just as we don't want to be derailed from making an exit off a highway, we don't want to be derailed from making choices that can change our life. We humans do not come equipped to know that deepest thoughts and intentions of each other so to create a human law that limits a specific group of people from following their own free will goes against the laws of the Universe. We don't know what our fellow humans came here to experience.

Some people will decide on abortion because it is in their highest and best interest, whether that be physical, mental, emotional, or spiritual in nature. Other people will make their choice for alternative reasons. The fact remains, however, the rest of humanity will never know their motive because the rest of humanity has not walked the same path, known the same joys or hardships, or look forward to the same experiences. Or, perhaps this *is* the experience their Soul came here to have. So, how can we judge, or dictate human laws in the presence of such ambiguity. We must trust that Source and the Universe does see the bigger picture, and then allow ourselves to be absolved from the burden of thinking we know what is the right choice for everyone else. When you comprehensively understand spirituality, you will no longer feel the need to modify another's choices.

Making your own choices is great, but keep in mind free will can also contribute to one's own challenging life. It allows us to make stupid mistakes, think ignorant thoughts, and walk down a foolish path, if that is where our decisions have led us. We rarely make these decisions knowing they are stupid, ignorant, or foolish. Free will lets us create/think/believe/do/be anything we want. Good or bad. And bad choices can lead to a less-than-perfect life. So, it may appear on the surface that we are here to learn or suffer, but that type of life is a result of our limiting beliefs and a long list of sketchy choices.

- Free will let you make poor food choices that led to poor health.
- Free will let you choose to marry a lazy, lying cheater, and now you're sad in your marriage.
- Free will let you goof off in school and now your being expelled.
- Free will let you chase riches and success, and now your wondering what other parts of life you missed out on.
- Free will let you decide to be aware of your gang, and so now you don't feel as if you walk this life alone.
- Free will let you choose to manifest positivity rather than think negative thoughts, and now your life is working out for you wonderfully.
- Free will has let you make all your choices up to now, thus creating the life you currently find yourself in.
- Free will can lead you to anything. Creativity, clarity, spirituality and transcendence, even personal ruin.

Karma

Now let's talk about karma in the context that most Westerners choose to understand it. Karma is the idea that you must somehow make up for all your bad deeds from a previous life (or an earlier part of this life) by suffering to some degree.

The Oxford Dictionary describes karma as "the sum of a person's actions in this and in previous states of existence, viewed as deciding their fate in future existences. The Sanskrit word for karma is *karman,* which means action, effect, fate."

Karma is not only reserved for the negative, bad, hateful, or unkind things you've done. Karma also works in the positive direction. For example, suppose you happen to cross paths with someone who is down on their luck and in need of money. You truly wish to help this person, so you generously give them one hundred dollars. According to karma, later that day or week you will find one hundred dollars while walking down the street or, in some unexpected way, money comes to you. The concept of the law of karma was originally from ancient India and has significance in Hindu, Buddhist, and other Eastern religions. The idea has also found its way into the Western culture and is even a household word. Whether Westerners actually believe it to be a law is doubtful, however, otherwise we would see many more people doing random acts of kindness, and less dishonorable, unscrupulous behaviors.

The other side of karma deals with bad choices and unsavory deeds. The following scenario depicts an example of how most Westerners think of karma: Your evening job is to steal cars from parking lots and sell them to a chop-shop for quick cash. A few weeks later, while sitting at a red light, your own car is involved in a hit-and-run accident, leaving you with a hefty repair bill and painful whiplash. Your hooligan friend chuckles and says, "Well, that's karma for ya!"

When we study karma alongside vibrational frequency and the Law of Attraction we can see how the idea of karma holds up. What you put out into the Universe will be what you get back. But do we need to *suffer*, or should we *experience*? Living a miserable existence because of the poor use of free will from another time does not resonate with foundational beliefs that stem from Love Energy. Is it possible to realize that a choice was wrong without having to suffer to get to this realization?

For example, if you were a rapist in a previous life, to make amends for your actions you may choose to be a support counselor for rape victims in this life. Or you may dedicate your life to being a detective who flushes out all the offenders of sex crimes.

If you cheated someone out of their fortune in a previous life, perhaps in this life you use your millions and billions in an altruistic manner by becoming a great philanthropist who touches the lives of many people in a positive way.

If you were a cranky, uncaring, bitter, and selfish pessimist before, and want to even out your karma in this life by sharing wonderful, positive energy, you could become a well-known comedian who brings joy, laughter, relief, and healing to others. Laughter is a great medicine for everything after all!

Do we need to wait until another lifetime to "even out the score," so to speak? Can someone who started a deadly fire on purpose decide to become a firefighter, risking his life for others in the same lifetime?

Karma can be repaid to others and to the Universe from a productive standpoint. The concept of "you need to suffer" is also so outdated. It's reminiscent of the eye-for-an-eye culture of long ago. If you were caught stealing, you would get your hand chopped off. There is no transfer of Love Energy that comes from suffering or inflicting suffering. We can imagine that the ultimate goal Source and the Universe would like to accomplish is beautiful, harmonious Love Energy that infuses all creatures, Souls, and situations. If you are made to suffer, when does the negative energy ever stop?

And what about the extreme cases? I recently heard a story about a father and his very young daughter. She was five years old. The daughter's friend came running to the father and told him something was wrong with his daughter as she pointed toward an old farm building off in the distance. The father dropped his tools and ran to the building with trepidation in his heart. As he approached, he heard his little girl screaming. He barged in and saw a man on top of her, holding her down. Both had no underwear on. The father, filled with an indescribable rage, beat the man to death with his fists.

In this story, the offender was punished and suffered at the hands of the father. There was no growth, no love or harmonious Love Energy. No chance for the offender to right his wrong. It was the classic example of an eye-for-an-eye. But was the father wrong? He reacted in a way that humans are emotionally designed to react. Karma will work within certain parameters but there are different degrees of bad decisions. When wicked, monstrous crimes are committed, all laws of the Universe are challenged. The Souls of wicked, monstrous offenders are managed by the Universe and Source in a way that ensures harmony. Karma may be a part of the harmony but it is not the entirety.

Even though we are Souls who wish to be creating, experiencing, and loving, we are also humans with innate instincts to protect and annihilate the evil around us. The father was not wrong in his actions. His genetic makeup dictated that he must protect his child. The force of energy that he absorbed from the UEF translated in his physical body as an unstoppable rage. Ultimately this father was not found guilty of any crime based on the laws of the state he lived in. What the offender faced after he left his body is certainly unknown to us, but the Universe requires balance.

And where should that balance begin? Remember, every action is almost always a reaction to an action that came before the reaction. And that action is also just a reaction to yet another action that came before it. And so on and so on and so on. Meaning, what happened to the offender to make him become an offender? Thankfully, the responsibility of creating balance is not ours.

A Hell Called Earth

Free will and manifestation play such a big role in our existence while incarnated. If you focus on negative thoughts and limiting beliefs, the life you lead and the world you live in will surely feel like a hell of sorts. As already stated, Source Energy, which eternally emanates Love, is Love and expresses Love in all It creates has no conscious, unconscious, or subconscious desire to inflict pain or suffering. Hell as described by religions is counterposed to the desires of Source and the Universe.

Biological Random Chance

What about the idea that humans accidentally came to be, and when it's over, it's over? Since this book is focused on spirituality, it is counterintuitive to give this theory much thought. Instead, let's reframe this to a more positive observation and include all the goodness in the world, all the synchronicities, unexplainable fortunate events, Love-based happenings, and answers to prayer. Is it pure luck? Is it coincidence? Synchronicities and mini-miracles happen to so many people! God winks are real, and it is your free will to interpret them any way you wish. For me, it's kind of like Source is giving us a wink every time a synchronicity or small miracle happens as if to say, "Hey there, you dear, sweet human Soul! I'm here with you. I'm watching you, and I'm helping you when you ask. Don't worry, you're not alone. You were never meant to do this alone."

Think About This

- If you had always known what your Soul's purpose was, would anything have been easier for you? Would you have made different choices?
- Reflect on the possible reasons we are here. Do any of them seem to resonate with you more than others? Which would you feel most confident explaining to someone else?
- Reflect on the story of the father and his young daughter. Most people would applaud the father for how he handled the situation he walked in on.
- Do you think the father violated the offender's free will?
- How would you have reacted in the same situation?

There is a beautiful movie (and book) called *The Shack* written by William P. Young, starring Octavia Spencer, Sam Worthington, and Tim McGraw. The story contemplates spiritual reckoning regarding these tough situations. I *highly* recommend it. Have you seen it? What parts of the story struck you the most?

- What are your thoughts on a fiery underworld called hell? Does this concept of hell stem from limiting beliefs that you were taught, or do you feel it is a fair description of a place where Souls who made poor choices could possibly end up?
- What are your limiting beliefs? Take time to think about it and be honest with yourself.
- Can you think of any limiting beliefs that you inherited from your parents, family, media or society?
- How are these beliefs helping you? How are they holding you back? How are they hurting other people?
- Do you think you can let go of these limiting beliefs? Why or why not?
- Can you think of any God winks that have ever happened to you? Keep a journal and write them down. Another fun way to record your synchronicities is to open a Google Docs page with a friend and each time a synchronicity happens to you, type it in the document and share it with your friend. In return they can write down their own synchronicities to share with you. This will inspire you to always be on the lookout for more winks.

NINE

GOALS, A PERFECT BODY, DEATH, AND THE JUDGE

More Clarity on Soul Goals

As Souls, we decided to incarnate into physical bodies to experience and create. Let's explore this a lot more deeply.

All Souls are a part of Source, and Source is the complete expression of All Love, All Good, All Knowing. But being a piece of something does not necessarily make it identical to that from which it came. For example, if a drop of water comes from the sea, that drop is still the sea. But does that drop hold within it every component that the entire sea has within it? Does a drop have every type of algae, organism, or even pollution within it? Does a drop contain the same amount of salt as all other parts of the sea? Does the same seaweed grow in every part of the sea, thus creating the same quantities of oxygen in every drop of the sea? The answer is *no!* But regardless of these differences in the sea, every single drop of water taken from the sea is still the sea!

A Soul brought forth from Source Energy is Source, but it cannot contain within it all infinite completeness that Source Energy has.

Does this mean a Soul is subpar? No, not subpar. But it is certainly on a journey to fill itself as completely and awesomely as the Source it came from.

A Soul's goal is to become as Source-like as possible. How Source-like can a Soul become? It can become very, very evolved until eventually it rejoins with the whole of Source Energy, but a Soul has a long, long journey before that happens. Generally speaking, if you, the Soul, have decided to manifest into physical form, then you are still seeking experiences, completeness, and oneness.

So, we are a Soul that occupies a body. The body (and Soul) come to the earth plane and physicality to create, love, experience, and become as Source-like as possible. The time spent in the body is very short compared to the eternity of the Soul, even if the body lives for a hundred years! Before incarnating, the Soul takes inventory of itself and decides what it would like to explore. The experiences to be had are countless, which is perfectly fine because we have countless lifetimes to expand ourselves. Sometimes experiences we set out to have never come to fruition. Rather, other experiences come into play because of things like free will, or absence of free will, or simply because once we got here to this earth platform we thought, *Oh hey! That other experience seems much more fantastic than what I originally planned out for myself! I think I'll go that way instead!* It's similar to getting in the car for a trip to the grocery store but on the way, you see a huge sale on shoes, and you start thinking, *To hell with the groceries! I'm getting shoes!* Of course you *need* groceries, but shoes would be so much more fun. So you make a little promise to yourself that next time you're out driving in your car you'll get groceries, but right now you want to do the fun thing and get *shoooees*! Unlike this example of shoes and groceries, the decision to change experiences is not made on a conscious level. Remember the concept of the veil that we have talked so much about, and the fact that we are not really aware of what our plan is? When thinking about it from that perspective, it's impossible to change your mind when you never really knew the plan to begin with.

We got off on another little tangent there, so let's bring this back to what our Soul intentions are. While preparing for a lifetime, the Soul can decide to choose experiences like:

- Perseverance
- Grace
- Orderliness
- Selflessness
- Compassion

- Forgiveness
- Purposefulness
- Tolerance
- Responsibility
- Altruism

- Generosity
- Wisdom
- Courage
- Respect
- Justice
- Self-Control
- Assertiveness
- Modesty
- Service
- Honesty
- Obedience
- Patience
- Leadership
- Truthfulness
- Moderation
- Courtesy
- Friendliness
- Loyalty
- Playfulness
- Sincerity
- Prayerfulness
- Greatness
- Docility
- Gratitude
- Industriousness
- Foresight
- Patriotism
- Meekness
- Tact
- Good Judgment
- Kindness
- Good Counsel
- Helpfulness
- And so much more!

These are all great virtues (or rungs on the ladder) that a Soul will be proud to master during its existence in physicality, and there are so many more than are listed here. Also, a Soul may want to fully realize *emotions* like:

- Sadness
- Disappointment
- Distress
- Rage
- Frustration
- Confusion
- Intolerance
- Loneliness
- Excitement
- Shame
- Anxiety
- Love
- Envy
- Jealousy
- Anger
- Resentment
- Joy
- Guilt
- Boredom
- Pridefulness
- Hopefulness
- Hopelessness

- Grief
- Serenity
- Freedom
- Moodiness
- Impatience

- Depression
- Happiness
- Humility
- Irresponsibility
- And many more

These are some very intense emotions! But the two most powerful emotions from which all other emotions are derived from are Love and Fear. Not love and hate. Hate is just a layer in the onion, and Fear is at the core. So let's pretend you're holding two onions. One is labeled Love and the other is labeled Fear. At the very center of the Love onion there is pure, Source-actualized Love Energy. The onion layers that sit on top of Love are other virtues that arise out of Love like goodness, generosity, hope, kindness, worthiness, friendliness, joyfulness, laughter, beauty, grace, mercy, peace, creativity, and so on. As you peel back the layers of this onion you see more and more descendants of Love. Look at your other hand and consider the Fear onion you are holding. It too is made up of layers, and at the very core of this onion you find Fear. The layers within this onion are lower-vibrating frequencies, some lower than others. Within it you find dishonesty, meanness, disregard, dishonor, malice, corruption, pervertedness, destruction, hate, wickedness, depravity, spitefulness, revengefulness, despair, anxiety, angst, doubt, worry, phobias, etc. When examining hate from a philosophical stance, one might think hate should reside at the core of the onion and be the polar opposite of Love, for what can be worse than hate and hate crimes? Well, let's peel back the layers from hate by using the example of "I hate women." (The "I hate women" example is so easy to use for this demonstration but the basic premise of going backward in your questioning can be used for any hate situation. You just have to be willing to do the work.)

-    — I hate women, and I have committed crimes against women.
- Why?
-    — They're all bitches.

- Why?
- They think they're entitled to anything they want. They manipulate. They lie. They're self-absorbed.
- Have you ever met a woman?
- Of course! I know tons of those bitches.
- Do you hate each one?
- Yes.
- Do you hate some more than others?
- Yes, some I hate more.
- Can you think of any you hate more than others?
- I hate all the ones in politics. Yep, especially the politicians.
- Why?
- Because they got big mouths, and no sense comes outta those mouths. Women should not be in power.
- What do you think they're trying to accomplish?
- Seems like they're trying to take over, manipulate, ruin us all. Women should never be in power.
- What would be wrong with them being in power?
- The country would go to hell.
- How?
- Who knows! They're all stupid.
- Have you ever been lied to or manipulated by a woman?
- Oh, sure! I've been screwed by those lying, hateful bitches.
- Which ones have lied to you?
- They all lie.
- Which woman has been the most hateful?
- They all are. Even my own mother!
- How did your mother hate you?
- Well, she used to whoop me good if I stepped out of line. I was just a little bitty boy, too.
- What else did she do?
- She'd beat me, scald my hands, lock me in the closet with no food. Wouldn't let me out till I told her I loved her. Do you see what I mean? They're all hateful.

- Did she love you?
- No, she did not!
- Where you scared when she did those things to you?
- Scared? I was petrified!
- Was she the first woman you knew?
- I suppose so.
- Did you fear her?
- Yes. I did fear her.

In this example, the origins of the man's hate for women has been illuminated. It is based in Fear Energy. Every thought or action can always be reduced back to its origins which is either Love or Fear.

Love Energy contains within it all things that are positive, some vibrating closer to Love than others.

Fear Energy contains within it all things that are negative, some vibrating closer to Fear than others.

It is very important to realize that Fear-based emotions propel other actions and free will decisions. It's equally important to understand why you feel the way you do about a thing or situation. Did you inherit the Fear-based beliefs from someone else? Or are you continuing to react from a time you had little knowledge, insight, wisdom, or education on a matter? Did you have an experience that left you with some degree of Fear? Having clarity on these questions is the first step to removing a low-vibrating emotion from your Chakra system. While it's true we came to experience all things, good and bad, we are not meant to feel uncomfortable feelings for the remainder of our physical lives. Holding on to the good feelings won't hurt you; in fact they are beneficial to you. But the bad feelings must be felt, experienced, understood, processed, and moved out. To constantly relive a negative experience every time it comes back into your conscious or subconscious awareness will only hurt you. Make peace with it, understand it for what it is, and let it go. Sometimes this work can be done on our own with complete success. Sometimes we need help from a coach or therapist who can act as a "life raft" to help us get our heads above the water long enough to see what's actually going on. This idea of needing to process out bad/negative emotions has been mentioned a number of times throughout the book because it is an important and key ingredient to physical health, emotional joy, and moving forward. You've got to embrace this idea.

During a lifetime, we can heavily concentrate on one or more experiences. Or we can choose a life in which we just sort of coast along, not really focusing on anything serious and enjoying all that physicality has to offer. And we can also decide to do any variation in between. The Soul (along with a spiritual team) carefully choreographs the life that will give it the best chance to experience the emotions or virtues it has chosen. But remember, the Soul also has free will, so the experience can be had in many ways. Some are more destructive than others.

Let's say in previous lifetimes the Soul never had a chance to fully embody the virtue of truthfulness and wants the experience of truthfulness in order to continue on its journey to becoming as Source-like as possible. How does experiencing truthfulness bring it closer to having the qualities of Source? Well, one cannot say that Source Energy doesn't understand the properties of truthfulness or what it feels like to be truthful, so having a deep, meaningful experience with truthfulness can bring the Soul one step closer to greater enlightenment, and onto transcendence. Let's take a look at the many different angles in which truthfulness can be experienced.

- You can lie.
- You can tell the truth.
- You can be lied to.
- You can be told the truth.
- You can be the victim of someone else's lie or truth.
- You can witness loved ones lying or being truthful.
- You can lose or gain because of truth or lies.
- You can be a role model for truth.

- You can be a motivating example to others on why lying is a poor choice.

The Soul (with the help of its gang) designs a specific life to best fulfill the prescribed goal, but that does not necessarily mean the life will be fun or easy. Perhaps the Soul chooses a scenario where it will lie or be deceitful, resulting in all loved ones abandoning the Soul as it carries out this experience in human form. Only then will the Soul fully appreciate the importance, advantages, and integrity that truthfulness can afford. And don't forget about free will. At any moment, a Soul can go off course or get back on course, thus allowing the experience to be more positive or negative, depending on the direction the free will took the Soul. There are many ways to fully explore and embody truthfulness. Perhaps another Soul would pick a much gentler scenario that still enables a profound experience. There are so many variables!

Some Souls even choose to be born with disease or physical disadvantages to fully embrace their chosen experience. I'm not implying all Souls who are born atypical have prearranged for their life to be this way. But because there are so many variables, we cannot assume to know the wise and grand plan of other Souls, Source, the Universe, and Spirit.

Understanding our Soul's intentions (and our Soul Goals) in this way can help ease heartache around unfortunate situations. We can begin to make a tiny bit of sense as to why a baby is born with what appears to be a disadvantage, or why children develop life-threatening diseases. We see pain and sadness, but the Soul of that child may be right where it needs to be to gain the wisdom it yearns for. And if you've ever spent time with a child who at first glance appears to be disadvantaged, you are well aware that this child is brimming over with other amazing gifts that may not have been accessible in a typical body.

People often wonder why bad things happen to good people. It's extremely hard to sit with peace and Love in our being knowing there are heinous crimes being committed. The family and friends of these victims are left with a hole ripped through their hearts, and sometimes it feels as if there is no loving thread that can mend those gaping holes.

When I was in eighth grade, a friend was brutally murdered in the wooded area next to our school. During the first four months after her murder, she was thought to be missing. Murder was never considered until finally her remains were found. Dental records confirmed her identity. Eventually the seventeen-year-old who murdered her was found and put in jail for twenty-five years. Like most murder cases, this was horrifying in every way imaginable. The community was shaken and devastated. Years later, I looked back on this moment and wondered if my friend's Soul choreographed her life to be murdered. What sense does that make? Where's the chance to create, love, and evolve as a Soul in this story?

There are so many experiences that we as Souls wish to partake in, and they may seem horrific from the human perspective.

As hard as it is to make sense of it, sometimes a Soul will set a life course with specific events that ultimately give others a chance to have an experience. A Soul can set up its lifetime in such a way that gives others the opportunity to go through emotions that will lead to profound experiences and realizations. In this case there were parents, siblings, family members, friends, teachers, police officers, neighbors, members of the community, the family of the offender, the offender himself, and many others who deeply experienced this tragedy.

It is also possible the free will of the offender unfortunately intersected with the path of the victim, resulting in an unplanned, unwanted removal from her body. Regardless of why death happens, it is always one of the most difficult emotions to experience for those left behind.

It is my hope that everyone eventually found peace emotionally from her passing. But as a parent myself, I acknowledge the fact that it can be a lifelong challenge to find solace and make sense of it all.

Even after years of Spiritual education, growth, clarity, and teaching, I still find it heart wrenching to know about these abhorrent crimes.

The individuals affected in this story did, however, have an opportunity to experience and expand on a massive level.

As for my friend, we can't help but wonder to what degree she suffered. It is the suffering and finality of it all that hurts those left behind after a loved one moves on, especially in this type of passing. After extensive meditating, intently listening to my Guides and mentors, listening to my own clairsentience and claircognizence, opening up to the UEF and settling in with what feels right, I have realized this: When a human is confronted with unimaginable pain, fear, or panic as a result of one's own free will being violated, the Grace of Spirit is instantly imparted to this person on a grand scale. It's as if a bubble of Love and protection actualizes over the person and Angels of Love swarm in. The individual's attention is acutely redirected to an out-of-body experience where the Soul is held in a protective energy of Love. The body may remain in the situation, but the consciousness does not always participate for the entire time. This Grace is given to any Soul that willfully accepts it and is not conditional to heinous crimes.

To fully understand how this works, let's go back to our little car analogy. You're driving down the road enjoying life, when you hear your cell phone alert you that a text has come in. You pull your car over to the side of the road to check your messages. Unbeknownst to you, you have pulled over and parked your car on a train track! Immersed in your text, you don't know a train is coming full speed about to smash into you. When you look up and see this train bolting down the tracks toward you, panic blasts through your mind and you're frozen with fear. But then, out of nowhere, a very kind and familiar face knocks at your window and calmly lets you know a tragedy is about to occur. (Remember, in this scenario, you and your car are equivalent to your Soul and your body.) You're told it would be best for you to get out of your car, and oh, by the way, look at those beautiful flowers over there. They smell like heaven.

The flowers *are* amazing, and you become completely transfixed on them. You're in awe of their beauty and their delicious smell, so you get out of your car and become completely focused on not only the flowers, but also this kind, familiar-faced person. You can *feel* the beauty and love from the flowers and *feel* the love from this person. Seconds after you get out of the driver's seat, the train hits and demolishes your car to pieces. The kind person shields you from debris as your car is destroyed.

As you look back, you are mostly unaffected because it's just a car, after all, and you can always get another one. There is no attachment to the car because the car is not you. The car is no longer important to you. Instead, the beautiful field of flowers ahead of you provides all the joy and love you need in that moment.

(In this story we are pretending there is no such thing as car insurance, lawsuits for parking on a train track, or a negligent train conductor. It happens to be one of those trains that operates itself by way of computer. Also, I'm sure you realized the kind, familiar face is your Guardian Angel.)

The example is a simplistic analogy of one way we can let go of our bodies in moments of violent chaos. Our loved ones, who must feel the unbearable weight of this experience, are not spared from the pain, however, and many more painful moments will still be yet to come from this experience. In time and through embracing their spirituality, loved ones can find a way out from under this weight and still be able to feel peace and joy. However, many people choose to stay under the weight, whether it be a conscious choice or not. They choose to stay in painful and sad darkness. That is their free-will choice. But please know that it is not a requirement to stay in this darkness forever. Sometimes after enduring such a heart breaking and painful experience, our minds seem to tell us we are required to remain in a state of mourning indefinitely. It's the part of the mind that, in other situations, tells you you're not good enough. It can emerge here too, insistently whispering into your ear, "How dare you be happy. You should be ashamed that you have let yourself experience joy again. Stay sad. It is the only way". Whatever the reason you can not pull yourself out of the darkness, know that it is ok to let go of that pain. Your loved one is still with you, blissful and surrounded by a Love Energy too powerful to understand by us as humans. This same Love Energy is also meant for you, even though these dark moments make it especially hard to feel. The light is always there for you … when you're ready.

Many years ago, I read a book called *Exploring the Eternal Soul* by Andy Tomlinson. It's a nonfiction book about a therapist who takes his patients on regression journeys to find answers they seek in regard to this lifetime. First, they travel back to childhood, then into the womb, then to their life between lives, and then into their past lives. There are so many fascinating stories from dozens of his patients. (Learning about life between lives, which is the time we are in Spirit as pure Soul energy, was incredibly fascinating.)

One story in particular that has stuck with me ever since I first read this book more twenty years ago is a regression of a woman who found herself in a past life as a child. She was a young girl, about the age of twelve or thirteen, in a concentration camp during World War II. It was Auschwitz. After the soldiers separated her from the rest of her family, she and her mother were herded into the gas chamber along with many other prisoners. Her mother was terrified beyond words. Everyone in the chamber knew they were about to die. In that moment the woman who was being regressed came to realize the purpose of her life in that lifetime. It was to be the love and strength her mother needed in her last moments. As the gas turned on, the young girl locked in to her mother's eyes with all the love and strength she was born with. Her love was able to bestow a calmness that carried her mother through that one solemn moment at the end, knowing her mother could not do it alone.

This story hits me on so many levels, but mostly I am in awe and inspired to know our Soul Goal can be as simple yet complex as showing up for someone in their most desperate moment. The smallest act of intently holding space and locking into someone's eyes and Soul to pour boundless, infinite, soothing Love Energy into their being is so incredibly profound. I really don't have the words to amply describe how remarkable it is.

I recognize there are a few grim examples in this book that are being used to illuminate spirituality as it pertains to our walk through life, but that's because they are powerful ways to convey a message. It's easy to know who we are and where we're going when life is great and there is so much happiness in every direction we look. It's in those times of devastation, fear, defeat and great sadness that we often cannot make sense of anything. The little car is trying to help you make sense of those things and remind you just how powerful you are.

My Vacation to Hawaii

My youngest daughter is quite an empath and has always felt the emotion of family, community and world events a bit more than what is considered normal. So when she was quite young and became aware of death, it hit her emotional meter like a storm. She became deeply upset about the notion that I could die. That's when I explained my Hawaiian vacation to her. But first, I asked her to remember the time we went on our trip to Disney. "Do you remember how exciting it was when we were getting ready to go? Do you remember how fascinated you were when we walked in and you saw all those enchanting sights? Do you remember how happy you were to be there? You had a fantastic time!" She agreed so I continued on.

"Now let's think about a trip just for me. I would love to go to Hawaii because it sounds like paradise. But what if, while I was packing for my amazing trip to paradise, you stood next to me, crying and crying? What if you said to me, 'Please don't go. I really don't want you to go.'? And at the airport, what if you stood by the window waving goodbye, sobbing because you were so sad to see me go?"

Big tears started to well up in her green eyes as she listened to me but I continued on with my teaching moment.

"I know I would feel just terrible about leaving. I know I would no longer be excited for my fabulous trip to Hawaii. I would regret that I was leaving. My adventure would no longer feel amazing and wonderful. But I'd still go because I would already have my tickets and people in Hawaii would be expecting me.

And what if when I got to Hawaii, you sent me letters every single day saying how very sad you are that I was gone? Would I be able to enjoy the paradise I was in? I don't think so because I would only be thinking about you the whole time and how very sad you feel. So if I ever go to Hawaii or Heaven, can you be happy for me? Can you say, 'Mama has finally gotten to go on that amazing trip she's always wanted! I'm so happy for her because she's in a beautiful paradise, and I know she's happy, and I know I'll see her again soon. And until I see her again, we can text a lot and maybe even call. Do you think you can say those things and be a little bit happy for me if I go on a trip?"

She thought for a moment while she wiped away the tears that now made a glossy trail down her little cheeks. Then, in her usual upbeat tone she said, "I think I can do that for you Mama, but only because I really love you."

The Hawaiian vacation story seemed to calm her young mind. After spending many, many more moments talking about spirituality with her, she is now able to take the idea of death in stride.

Try to give your loved one who has passed the best gift you can give, all your love and happiness.

Sara's Story

Sara shared her story with me as I was finishing writing this book. After hearing it, I knew it had to be included because the entirety of her story is going to be the God wink that some readers need. It is going to be the words that bring some readers from a place of dark sadness to illuminated peace.

Hanalei was a Miniature Schnauzer. She was named after a beach in Hawaii and she was Sara's best friend. Together they walked through life, and their love for each other was timeless. Anyone who has ever had a pet can easily resonate with this feeling, but according to Sara, Hanalei was more compelling than any other dog she knew. She had a way about her that inspired Sara to love life, herself, and everyone she met with a joyful zest. As each other's best friend, they had a spiritual connection that will never end.

After 10 years together, Hanalei's time in physicality was coming to an end and after making an agonizing, heart-wrenching decision, Sara made the choice to bring her to the emergency vet for a final act of compassion and love. She was grief-stricken and it felt as if a deep gash was splitting her heart in two. Sara said to me, "I'll never forget that moment when I was holding my dog's limp and lifeless body in my arms after she was euthanized. I was sobbing and in shock, but suddenly, I felt compelled to look up. I saw the most brilliant ball of light hovering in front of me, over my little dog's body!" Sara tried explaining to me what this ball of light looked like but she said words can not explain the complexity and beauty of what she saw. It was slightly larger than a baseball and it emanated white light. Within the white light was a profusion of different colors swirling and merging through each other. She said it was the most beautiful thing she had ever seen. The ball of light stayed fixed in one spot but the colors inside moved very quickly. There even seemed to be objects inside the ball but because everything moved at what appeared to be light speed, it was impossible to know what these objects were. Then something amazing happened.

Sara felt as if she was moving into the light and then down a long hallway or corridor of sorts. In this space she began to feel an all encompassing presence of absolute Unconditional Love. At this point as Sara spoke, she paused again to emphasize how our conventional use of the word "love" did not even come close to what she was feeling. It was a feeling beyond love, beyond anything that exists in the physical realm. She searched for a way to more accurately describe the euphoric feeling she had found herself in but could not. She said the word love seemed cheap and grossly inaccurate compared to the level of love she felt.

In this moment she began to become aware of a Universal Law. Perhaps she was opening up to a greater part of the UEF thus absorbing more of what the Universe had to offer. The law, as she understood it, said "Love is the greatest power in our Universe and beyond. Unconditional Love is the basis for all there is and it will be all there ever is forever and ever." Sara said according to her understanding, that which appears evil to us as humans will eventually revert back to love. This seemed to be a firm and absolute law.

From this amazing experience, she suddenly found herself engulfed in another profound moment. Sara felt the sensation that she was floating. Then she felt layers of emotions shed away from her being. Feelings like guilt, shame, sadness, conditioning, anger, frustration, and many other emotions that weighed her down throughout her life lifted away and dissolved from her energy field all at once. She said, "I have never felt more light, more free, more seen, more known, more understood, more unconditionally loved, and more accepted exactly as I am to the very core of my being than I did in that moment. We don't realize the heaviness and conditioning that we carry here on earth every second of every single day. We don't realize this heaviness comes from our thoughts, experiences, and beliefs. We may as well be dragging around an invisible five hundred pound ball and chain."

Sara's entire encounter was void of any fear. She felt no judgment against her. She knew every part of her consciousness was exposed, every action taken or word spoken throughout her life was exposed. But still, there were no feelings of judgment against her. The feeling of being wholly accepted and loved was beyond anything she had ever felt in her human existence. To be in the presence of such enormous, magnificent Love was an incredible gift because she realized that it was within this Love Hanalei now resided. Sara said, "If we all could feel this Love, even for a second, we would never mourn anyone who passes in the same way again. We would know, without a doubt, that they continue existing in this realm of pure, unconditional, absolute Love. Cared for in perpetual bliss."

This experience made Sara realize with complete certainty there is no such thing as death, only changing form. She expressed with great confidence there is no need to fear death and when her time comes to go back to the realm of energy, she looks forward to the euphoric peace centered in the heart of Love. That said, loosing your best friend is still hard to do. While we continue here on earth, there remains an emptiness where that friend used to sit. From this perspective, it really hurts. Even with the knowledge that our loved ones are in the most amazing state of bliss that is unimaginable to us, we miss them. Never again will we hear their laughter, see their smiles, or feel their touch. But that does not mean they are gone. They still interact with us and are well aware of how very sad we are. Perhaps we should not dwell in sadness and let them enjoy this new adventure they have set out on! Knowing we are in misery because of their exit from physicality will only interfere with their own moments of joy. They are here, they will always be close to us. We just need to learn how to experience our loved ones from a different vantage point, and that starts with knowing who *we* are beyond *our* physical body.

Sara is not sure how long these unforgettable moments lasted, maybe a few minutes. Then, without warning, her consciousness was fixed back in the veterinarian's office. The hovering light shot across the room and disappeared through a wall. That was her last physical encounter with what she believes was Hanalei's Soul. Smiling, Sara said, "Hanalei was quite a charming little dog. I do believe she could have pulled some strings and, with Spirit's help, allowed me the greatest gift ever, a glimpse into where our Souls go after they leave our physical body. Unconditional Love is the greatest power in the Universe. It is our Soul connection to Source Energy. Love never dies."

Your Body Is Perfect

Now let's talk a little bit more about how your Soul (you) had input on how your body would look for you to have the experiences it wanted to have. Your Soul is well aware of the bigger picture, especially before it put itself into the body. It (you) knows the best way it (you) should look for it (you) to have the most complete experience it (you) came here for. That doesn't unequivocally mean your ultimate plan is to keep that body just as it is. Here is one example to highlight this point.

Some Souls come into their lives assigned as male or female and then choose a gender transition. Obviously, there are infinite reasons a Soul would see value in this experience. To explain the statement from chapter one, "Realize that no matter what you look like, you look perfect! You look exactly the way you (Soul) wanted to look in order to have the experience you thought would best serve you in this time." I will suggest one possible desired experience among many others: the experience of exercising true expression.

A Soul may be seeking an experience of exercising its ability to truly express itself, even in the face of judgment, pain, and abandonment. This is a very heavy experience, and one that can probably only be taken on by a Soul who has had some amount of preparation in previous lifetimes. The desire to transition isn't decided on a whim. It comes from an unrelenting desire to be what you know you should be. Sadly, it can come at a cost. Being judged by society, enduring the pain of surgery, suffering loss, and experiencing abandonment from loved ones who could not honor a Soul's free will or see beyond the surface and into the beauty of a Soul are all excruciating experiences that the Soul is well aware of. But even in the face of all this, the need to experience true expression is the greater force. Judgment, pain, and loss can be so heart wrenching, and can even supersede the original experience the Soul set out to have. For all these reasons, many Souls will not choose this experience because it is so intense. For those Souls who do choose to take on this experience, they do so to journey closer to the conscious awareness of oneness.

Or could this experience be the first step to a more accepting and beautiful future for our world? People who choose a gender-affirming surgery are brave pioneers leading the way to teach the rest of us that the body is not who we really are!

Their message is, "Look at my Soul! That's who you're interacting with! Why are you so concerned about the vehicle I travel in? Why are you not able to look into my eyes and see me for who I am really am? My eyes are the windows to my Soul. I am so much more than what you let yourself see."

The body is just the vehicle. What it looks like is insignificant compared to how the Soul shows up. How we decorate or change these bodies is personal preference. Why should it matter to anyone else? Do you care how many bumper stickers I put on my car? Do you really care what I hang from my rearview mirror? Or what kind of hubcaps I choose? Or what color paint I pick for the exterior? Or if I put a cap on the back of my truck? Or if I attach a trailer to the back? Or how messy my back seat is? As long as it doesn't hurt anyone or anything else, as long as it doesn't interfere with another's free will, it doesn't matter.

Your body is just a vehicle. Your Soul is the eternal quintessential epicenter of you!

Louis

We've laid so much groundwork so far. The foundational concepts have been presented. At this point you should be starting to feel yourself as quite an extraordinary being compared to when you first picked up this book. Now you need to put it into action. Decide how you want to be seen and how you want to feel. Take inventory of yourself. Accept the belief that you are allowed to have complete happiness today, right now. You don't have to wait! If that feels uncomfortable or wrong, there are emotions that you must still acknowledge and let go of.

Here is another example of Soul Goals and deciding to embrace happiness. Let's look at the story of a wonderful, devoted father named Louis.

Louis was in an icy, sullen relationship with his wife. Every day together was a struggle and an argument. They both knew staying together could not be an option, as the joy of life was slowly but surely draining from their hearts. Louis and his wife decided to divorce. That decision was easy compared to what came next. The couple had two small children whom he adored. They were his life. Everything Louis did was for the children. Ever since they were babies, he would sing them songs, make up stories to tell them at bedtime, and cook them breakfast every morning. He taught them to tie their shoes, ride their bikes, and how to swim. Together they built a lemonade stand, and they even made up their own version of the Mocking Bird song. If they had a nightmare, he would come running and hold them in his arms until they fell back to sleep. If they were hurt or sick, he was the one who nursed them back to health. Louis worked hard at his job but was able to arrange his hours so that he was there for his kids as much as possible. He spoke to me about them with such adoration, never leaving out any details. The love he had for them was endless. Good times or bad, they were the joy of his life. When the divorce became a reality, the child custody arrangement meant that Louis had to be separated from his children every other week. He said the feeling of parting with them for an entire week was excruciating. The children would cry and hold tightly to his legs begging him in their tiny voices, "No, Papa, please! I stay with you!" His heart tore into pieces as he held back burning tears. Every week for years the same agonizing moment played out as they left with their mom, which was immediately followed by a week of depression for Louis.

As he grew spiritually, Louis's heart started to mend, and he was able to let go of the experience of being severed from his children. Instead of holding on to the heartache he endured, he looked to the good times he shared with his children. He said he chose to not be defined by the days of misery he felt when he was removed from them. Instead, he chose to be defined by the days filled with joy when they were together. As he started to tell a new story to himself, he gradually noticed that the time he spent apart from them started to become easier. He looked for new ways to enjoy his life, making sure he didn't allow guilt to creep in. He was clear in his mind that nothing would ever replace the children, but he knew it was important to be happy. He knew it served no one to feel guilty about being happy in those weeks they were separated. It took time to allow himself to accept happiness in the children's absence, but eventually he did.

What Louis's Soul wanted to experience in this situation could have been any number of things. Separation, loss, lack of control, victimization, emptiness, pain of losing a child, disempowerment, fear, sorrow, self-pity, panic, depression, anguish, or any other variety of pain that is experienced in the Heart Chakra or Solar Plexus Chakra. He said he thought he probably experienced all of them at one time or another!

In Louis's darkest moments, he turned to Jesus and Mother Mary for help and soothing. As a Catholic, these two entities helped pacify the pain he felt. He said he always had a close connection with Jesus, and he also wanted to turn to Mary because she must've known how he felt since her own son had been taken from her.

When you focus on positive Love Energy, positive Love Energy will attract itself back to you, regardless of where you choose to find that Love Energy.

If the Soul Goal is to become as Source-like as possible, we must know what the good *and* the bad feels like. Source Energy is the All. Would the All not know what sorrow feels like? Could you say Source doesn't understand what it feels like to be cheated, abused, abandoned, alone, sick, confused, lost, scared, lied to, angry, greedy, lacking, relentless, selfish, insincere, unforgiving, intolerant, unthankful? No, you could not. Source energy understands all of this.

When we fully engage in certain experiences that bring us to feeling emotions like helplessness and emptiness, we often look to Source and Spirit to support and guide us through it. What if Source had no reference point, no knowledge of what these emotions felt like? Talk about feeling like you're out on an island all by yourself! Luckily, Source does know how all these emotions feel. All of Spirit does. We are never alone, no matter how dark it feels. We are not meant to go through challenging life experiences alone. We are not meant to go through the joyful experiences alone either! Share those moments with Source and Spirit! They want to love us in all ways. In our darkest moments *and* in our brightest.

Remember, the Soul's life is eternal. Your time in this life is very short when compared to your Soul's infinite existence. When you start to see yourself as a Soul, and not as the body that you dress in clothes and move about on the earth in, you will start to realize there is a so much more going on than just the day to day in our physical world.

When you are a part of complex, difficult experiences and emotions, you (your Soul) are doing what you (your Soul) set out to do. You're living the experiences you planned for this lifetime. But remember, it does not have to go on forever. When you feel the experience has gone on long enough, free will lets you move on! Raise your vibrational frequency, start telling yourself a new story, see the bigger picture, know who you are beyond your physical body, call on your gang for help, live in the moment! But don't do nothing. Don't fall deeper into the darkness. The first steps always feel like the toughest, but you have the strength you need. You've got this!

Before Louis decided to change his thoughts and his story, the pain really started affecting his Chakras, specifically his Heart Chakra, because he continued to feel the emotion for years. His

Heart Chakra was starting to grow an energetic wall around it, and he was having great difficulty enjoying any part of life. Physically, his lungs were showing signs of poor health. Happiness was out of reach because his Heart Chakra was compromised, and it wasn't interacting with the UEF. All of life around him seemed gray and like a chore that had no end. As time went on, he allowed himself to have a greater perspective. In doing so, he grew spiritually and had realizations that enabled him to let go of the pain. With help and a lot of hard work, he left the emotions in the past. When he did this, happiness found its way into his life and his kids benefited from it. By showing them he had Love Energy, they found it much easier to accept Love Energy for themselves.

This is a wonderful example of an individual experiencing emotions that allow the Soul to continue its journey to become as Source-like as possible, then letting the emotions go back to the past where they belong. Louis will never forget what he went through. But he knows he doesn't have to relive those painful emotions again and again. Instead, he fills that space with Love.

This is also a wonderful example of halting a limiting belief. Louis showed his children the magnificence that was attainable by letting an abundance of Love Energy into his awareness and into his being. If Louis did not change his outlook, a very unfortunate limiting belief could have been created in his family system.

It's also important to recognize that Louis's Soul did not *only* choose a challenging experience, it also chose the experience of family love. He fully experienced deep love and affection with his children. Our lives are made up of so many experiences, but it's so easy to focus intently on the heavier, more challenging experiences. One of the exercises for raising your vibrational frequency is to be grateful. When you bring your focus to the good things in your life, you will start to realize there are many good things happening. Don't lose sight of them! Your Soul (you) wanted to experience the good also. If you can't find these positive things through the heavy darkness, just start with something simple. You're bound to find a cheery experience in nature, so if you just can't find anything anywhere else in your life, start with nature. Then let the momentum build from there. You've got this! I know you do.

Don't Judge Me!

> Do not judge my story by the chapter you walked in on.
> —Unknown

> Life is not a school but an experience. Don't judge those who chose a different experience from yours.
> —Jennifer Merritts

> Do you have the right to judge another?
> Do you have the wisdom to judge another?
> Do you have the time to judge another?
> Do you have the experience to judge another?

We have talked a lot about incarnating into a human body and having a variety of experiences over many different lifetimes to know Source more intimately. Moving up the ladder of spiritual evolution is something we Souls are dying to do. (LOL, pun intended!)

In grade school, all the kids in a class are learning the same material and moving along at relatively the same pace. In regular life, however, it does not work that way at all! We have all chosen to have different experiences for very specific reasons, and therefore we are *not* all moving along at the same pace.

In second grade, students are given the same list of spelling words to learn and the same math problems to solve. After learning them, they are tested to ascertain who has mastered the concepts of reading, addition, and subtraction and who has not. All the concepts to learn are the same.

Outside of school we are all going at a different pace. When you take into consideration the many experiences that a Soul can choose to have, and the many lifetimes a Soul can have to actualize these experiences, it doesn't seem feasible, plausible, or practical for all Souls to have the same experiences at once. Can you image if 7.6 billion Souls chose to incarnate at roughly the same time to experience leadership? All generals and no privates. All CEOs and no workers. All Batmans and no Robins.

How about a world full of people experiencing confusion? More than 7.6 billion people walking around aimlessly, scratching their heads or in therapy. The therapists would be useless because they would be just as confused! It would be a world full of Homer Simpsons.

How about vanity?

Gluttony?

Greed?

Depression?

Ooh! What if everyone wanted to experience kindness all at once? Nope, that wouldn't work either. All you would hear people saying is, "What do you want to do?"

"I don't know, what do *you* want to do?"

"Whatever you want to do."

"But I want *you* to be happy, so what do you want to do?" Over and over and over!

Everyone engaging in the same experience at the same time would lead to an unproductive, dysfunctional society where people would have a very hard time actuating their experiences. We *need* people to be different from one another, to experience at different intervals and be a variety of people. Once we master an experience, it will then be easily recalled upon from within our Soul during this or future lifetimes, if we choose.

It is ridiculous to think we are all moving along the same timeline and participating in the same ventures from the same vantage point. You may have not yet mastered what I have already experienced and assimilated into my being. And what you understand very clearly, I may still have yet to know. We all move along at a different pace. We all interact with the UEF at different levels and invite in frequencies that we are ready to receive. Remember, there is so much the UEF has to offer, but we are aware of parts of its endless knowledge and wisdom at distinctly precise moments that don't necessarily match up with how and when other Souls bring that information into their awareness. This is similar to what Jane and Amanda struggled with, remember? We go at our own pace. It's not a race! Therefore, it is absurd to think you can judge another Soul. Life situations that seem like quite a hardship to you may be easy for me to overcome, and events that are heavy and unbearable for me may have no effect on you. It all depends on what we as Souls have already experienced to completion, and which parts of the UEF resonate with us.

Experiences start at the very beginning of our lives and never stop. They cause us to have diverse opinions, and they cause us to react to each other in varying ways. There's not just *"the right way"* and *"the wrong way"* to view the details of humanity, *there are millions of ways.*

Below are some experiences that most likely will be felt and processed uniquely, depending on who we are and where we have come from. Each one adds another layer onto a person's identity and contributes to how they make choices going forward. Whether it's a stranger, family member, or a twin sibling, the whole of an experience will be processed and metabolized from a vantage point based on the layers of experiences that came before it. Remember this next time you encounter a stranger when you're walking through a public place. Don't quickly react to their behaviors from a negative perspective and then feel that knee-jerk reaction to judge them. Instead, remind yourself that everyone has a story, everyone comes from somewhere, everyone is doing the best they can with the information they have available to them ... just as you are.

Read the following ordinary and extraordinary experiences that are possible in anyone's life. As you go through the list, answer the questions as they pertain to you, but then also think about alternate answers that could be given to each question. The intent of this exercise is to realize that as humans we have so many experiences. Because these experiences are diverse and personalized, they can and do change how we react to what comes next for us. No two people can possibly be the same; we all have unique backgrounds that make us react within all degrees of the human spectrum. Think about each question and decide if you would show up differently in this lifetime if your answer varied from what it actually is.

1. What was your experience in the womb?
2. What year, month, day, were you born?
3. Was your birth difficult when you entered this world?
4. Was your family happy to receive you when you were born?
5. Were you nurtured and loved as a baby?
6. Are you male, female, both, neither?
7. Do you/did you play sports?
8. Were you raised by a parent or grandparent, or were you adopted or raised in an orphanage?
9. Did your childhood have consistency?
10. Did you feel safe as a child?
11. Did your parents divorce?
12. Are you divorced?
13. Did your spouse die?
14. Did/do you have many friends?
15. What kind of schools did/do you go to?
16. Was your family rich, poor, or somewhere in between?
17. What part of the world did you live in while growing up?
18. Was this part of the world safe?
19. Do you still live in this place?
20. How many times did you move?
21. Are you allowed to have control over yourself?
22. Have you live through tragedies?
23. What injuries have you suffered throughout your life?
24. Have you ever had a disease?
25. Do you have sight and hearing?

26. What injustices have you endured?
27. Were you/are you considered beautiful?
28. Were you encouraged as a child and teenager?
29. Were you beaten down mentally?
30. Were you beaten down emotionally?
31. Were you beaten down physically?
32. Were you born with a disability?
33. Did you develop a disability?
34. Are you loved?
35. Are you ignored?
36. Did you work at a job as a teenager?
37. Do you have a job now?
38. Do you get paid a salary?
39. Do your boss and coworkers value you?
40. Is there anyone you can go to in your life for guidance?
41. Have you always had access to information?
42. Do you come from a big family?
43. Did someone you love die?
44. How old were you when someone you loved died?
45. Do you wish you had children?
46. Do you have children?
47. Do you wish you didn't have children?
48. What's your sexual preference?
49. Does your gender fit you?
50. Is your sexual orientation accepted in your family?
51. Is your sexual orientation accepted in your community?
52. Have you suffered abuse?
53. Have you abused someone?
54. Do you have talents?
55. Are you allowed to express your talents?
56. Are you physically big, small, or average?
57. Were you ever in a war?
58. What race are you?
59. What nationality are you?

60. What religion are you?
61. Is your background accepted in your community?
62. Are you healthy?
63. Are you brave?
64. Did you experience an abortion?
65. Do you have a pet?
66. Is your family famous (or infamous)?
67. Do you love nature?
68. Do you prefer cities?
69. Do you have someone to share your feelings with?
70. Do you laugh easily?
71. Are you introverted?
72. Are you pro-choice or pro-life?
73. Do you believe in equality for all people?
74. Is music important to you?
75. Are you vegetarian or carnivore?
76. Do you engage in social media?
77. Do you live in the moment, regret the past, or worry about the future?
78. Were you ever incarcerated?
79. Do you feel heard?
80. Is there anyone in this world you fear?

Any number of these experiences (and, as you are well aware, there are so many more than are listed here), as well as combinations of them, are factors that can, and do, change how people react to situations. So how can we judge one another when we don't know what it is that we are judging? How can we judge one another when our inventory of experiences have so little in common with someone else's?

To be the judge of a dance competition or a cooking contest you must be an expert in that field. You must have at some point mastered dance or the art of cooking. At that point, you may be considered expert enough to judge someone else, but only in that arena.

You should know that if you are on this earth, incarnated into a body, engaging in your own experiences, you have not yet traveled high enough on the spiritual ladder. Therefore, you are not in the least bit qualified to judge the actions, values, or lifestyle of someone else if they are not hurting or interfering with another. Furthermore, if you are here, you are no expert and therefore you are not eligible to judge anyone, *ever!*

Judging also lowers your vibrational energy, making it much harder for you to be a powerful energy being, a topic we are about to embark on.

If you judge, it can be one of the worst mistakes you ever make. Remember all of this as you engage with family, friends, or individuals unknown to you.

Think About This

Can you think of any emotions or situations you have gone through that may have brought you up the spiritual ladder to become more Source-like?

What is the most traumatic event that has ever happened to you or continues to happen to you? This could be something from your early childhood or from more recent times. Try not to dwell on this question for too long. Remember, it's not about reliving the emotions, it's about letting them go.

Are you able to leave the emotional pain in the past? Do you carry it with you?

Look back on the lists of emotions and virtues from the section called More Clarity on Soul Goals. Do any of them resonate with you as something you think your Soul (you) would like to experience (or are experiencing) in this lifetime?

Refer back to the list of eighty experiences. Get together with a group of friends or relatives and ask those questions to the group. Record your findings. Tally how many individuals have the same answers. Of the people who have Most or All the same answers as you, would you say they view life exactly the same way you do with no exceptions?

All (80) of the same answers _____

Most (41-79) of the same answers_____

Half (40) of the same answers_____

Very few (fewer than 39) of the same answers_____

None of the same answers_____

Yes or No

Do you all live very similar lives? _____

Do you all have similar values?_____

Can you decipher if any one of your answers was the catalyst that changed any of your other answers?

Do you all have the same health? _____
(Remember, how you process emotions will directly affect your Chakras, which directly affect your health.)

Do you feel any of the above experiences have held you back or continue to hold you back from creating the life you want? If so, how can you change that?

Are you pleased (or displeased) to have had these experiences because you feel they led you to be who you are today?

Do you like who you are today?

Can you think of any other experiences not listed that impacted who you are today?

TEN

CATS BARKING AND SNOWBALLS MELTING

What Is a Thought?

Knowing who you are on a spiritual level is a very important part of learning how to become a powerful energy being. Just as you cannot be a world-famous chef until you know your way around the kitchen, you cannot fully create energetically until you know who you are beyond your physical body. Now that we have explored the Soul, Chakras, the UEF, limiting beliefs, vibrational frequency, and other concepts, it's time to understand how to actually create what you want. And the first concept to visit is *thought*. The power of thought gives us the ability to create and, therefore, have anything we desire. By putting all of our attention, intention, and direction into a very specific idea, we can ultimately manifest that idea into physical action. So, as you can see, understanding thought can be very useful and powerful.

Go through the next few paragraphs slowly. Take them in small bites. Like everything else presented thus far, we will be breaking these concepts down into easy-to-use steps.

Everything in the Universe is energy, even thoughts. In 1905 Albert Einstein shared what is now a well-known equation, $E = mc^2$, which in simplistic terms means that energy and mass are transposable. They are the same thing, only in different forms. This equation helped spur the Manhattan Project and atomic bombs, followed by nuclear reactors (which Einstein did not participate in). Proving the reverse of his equation seemed a little more difficult until 2014, when a group of scientists from Imperial College London and a visiting physicist from Germany figured out how to turn energy directly into matter. Using a tin can, photons, and light like the light emitted by stars, these scientists agreed they should be able to detect the formation of electrons and positrons as they exited the can. This is wonderful news for the scientific community. At the time this news was published, the race to carry out and complete the experiment was on.

The actualization of turning energy to matter in a laboratory is impressive, yet complicated, especially when scientists are trying to do it without the assistance of Universal Energy. Turning our thoughts into reality is equally impressive but not quite as complicated. So let's talk about harnessing this creative power also known as manifesting!

Have you ever tried to make a cat bark like a dog? It's doubtful, because you know the real energy needed to make a bona fide, lifelike dog barking sound only comes from a dog. Cats do not tap into the same energy required to produce a bark. That said, in time, with patience, training, and with the right cat, you may eventually be able to get a little woof-like sound out of a cat. But that sound doesn't have the authenticity of a real dog bark for one main reason ... the cat is not a dog. Using that analogy, can you see how trying to force energy to become matter in a laboratory using a laser, electrons, protons, and a tin can (all of which are void of intentional Love Energy or a direct connection to Source and Universal Energy) can make the experiment less climactic than when we as Soul Energy partner with Source Energy and Universal Energy to create anything we desire? There is ease and grandeur in creating when we are connected to these energies that we have a natural affinity to. Trying to force a creation without already being tapped into this energy will result in an unremarkable creation.

Energy cannot be created or destroyed, but it can change from one form to another. When you have a thought or a desire, you must realize that it is existing in the form of energy. The more often you think about that thought, the more energy accumulates around it, like a snowball rolling down a hill, getting bigger and bigger as it picks up more snow along the way. To manifest a thought into physical existence, your job is to give the thought unlimited positive attention and nurture the energy until it changes from energy to matter or a physical interaction. As it becomes activated with more energy, and more details of what you desire begin to take shape in your thoughts and within the Universe, you start to bring that goal, that ideal, closer to your reality. In the realm of energy your thoughts start to build by way of vibrational frequencies. As the vibrations attract other similar energetic vibrations, expansion continues until ultimately you create what you want in its physical form.

Have you ever seen someone developing pictures in a darkroom? As the solution washes over the paper, you begin to see a very vague representation of the image. As moments go by and the developing chemicals do their work, the blank paper starts to show a vague image. With more time a defined image appears where before there was just the suggestion of one. When you try to create using your thoughts and intention, the same gradual development happens. But if you take the picture out of the chemicals too soon or add in the wrong chemicals, the development stops. The same happens if you stop focusing on your desire, or if you let negative thoughts come in. The manifestation comes to a halt.

The photo example is not literal though. Your own manifestation project will not develop in the same way. Suppose you've decided it's time for a new car and you give this a lot of thought. You're beginning to manifest. The car is not going to start its appearance as a translucent, shadowy figure or apparition and then slowly become more tangible, more physical until it's suddenly there! On the contrary, when you create with the power of thought, the Law of Attraction is applied and a vibrational frequency from the Universe that matches the vibrational frequency of your thought is attracted to the energy of your thought. Eventually, that frequency attracts more of itself until it has manifested from energy form to physical possibility. The ability for you to have the new car goes from an impossibility to a possibility. The "how" part of that process is not important. "How will you get that new car if you don't have the money to buy a car?" Details like that are for the Universe to maneuver. A series of events will unfold and lead you to a new car because that was the direction of your energy. That was the only energy you attracted toward yourself. You were focused and your focus is the outcome (a new car). How the Universe orchestrates the "chess moves" necessary for the realization of a new car is not your worry. If you allow vibrational frequencies of doubt into your thought process, it will take much longer for you to accomplish your goals. You must leave doubt out of it. If we agree on the example that vibrational frequency connecting to your energetic thoughts is like a snowball rolling with momentum, picking up snow as it rolls, then doubt is like hot water being poured on that snowball. Any advances toward manifestation melt away.

This may seem like a lot to digest at first. But if you can accept the following flow, you will know the most important parts.

- Energy from the Universe is available for you to do with as you desire.
- You can activate this high-vibrating energy when it matches your thoughts.
- The more attention you give this thought, the more real it can become (provided you cultivate it with unshakable, positive attention and intention that it void of doubt).
- The Law of Attraction steps in and provides the remaining ingredients needed to give your thought real power, because the Law of Attraction states that "like attracts like."
- With time, your thought can manifest into the outcome you desire. How much time does it take? That's up to you and your ability to focus on your goal. Don't let others shake you off your path. There is *always* going to be somebody who says, "It can't be done." "It's a long shot." "What if you fail?" Limit your time with these people. They are not helping you! They are most likely very unhappy or fearful in their own lives and would like nothing more than for you

to join them. People who focus on the negative will attract more negative. It can go both ways. Whatever you focus on, whatever you give your attention to is what you will manifest into your life.

A client once told me she was not able to manifest anything positive. She talked a lot about things she didn't like, her misfortunes, the sad state of the world, and political disappointments from her perspective. I highlighted for her the fact that she focused too much on these negative things. She replied by saying, "Well, I don't want these negative things, so why is the Universe giving me more and more of it?" I explained that the Universe only matches what you focus on. It doesn't matter if you want it or not. What matters is what you focus on.

ELEVEN

HARNESS THE POWER — IT'S EASIER THAN YOU THINK

Five Steps to Harnessing Powerful and Creative Energy

Thought. Clarity. Visualize. Positivity. Make It Happen.

How, exactly, do we transform our thoughts into tangible matter so that we can experience them in our physical reality?

The earth is where we are. It's our playground to experience *and* create. *So shouldn't we have what we want in the here and now?*

How do we do that?

The process is so simple that it can seem too simple. As humans, we tend to overcomplicate things. We tend to think anything of worth and value requires hard work (a limiting belief). If it's more expensive, it's probably better. If the process is simple, it's probably a gimmick. But when it comes to being a powerful energy being, we will reach our goals quicker when we let go of the limiting belief that it needs to be complicated (or any other limiting belief you subscribe to that slows you down).

In addition to the five steps that you will follow below, it is also important to activate everything else learned so far.

- Identifying your limiting beliefs
- Overcoming your limiting beliefs
- Understanding the advantages of meditating
- Meditating daily
- Understanding your Chakra system
- Releasing emotions that create imbalance
- Connecting with the true essence of who you are (your Soul)

- Being aware of the UEF
- Letting go of habits that lower your vibrational frequency
- Creating habits that raise your vibrational frequency

When you use all the information you have learned, you will have tremendous ability to create what you want. You will start to manifest the changes and desires you want.

Here's a step-by-step guide to harnessing powerful and creative energy:

- Step 1. Think of something you want to have in your life. It should be something that is important to you. Be very clear with yourself about what you want to create.

If you don't have a clear mental picture of what you want, it will be much harder to send the vibrational frequency of what you desire out to the Universe. Remember, you don't have to see it as a clear mental photograph in your mind's eye, but you must have a clear awareness of what it is. Exactly what you send out to the Universe is exactly what the Universe will focus on. This means if you don't have a clear intention, you will not get precisely what you want. Being very clear with yourself first is extremely important.

If you are not one hundred percent clear on what you want or you're having trouble visualizing it, try making a vision board. A vision board is just a poster board or a white board that has representations of your goals and desires. Cut pictures from a magazine, use your own photos, tape receipts to the board. Stick sticky notes with quotes or ideas to it. Anything you want for yourself goes on the board. Over time, you will start to see a clear picture of what makes you the most happy.

- Step 2. When you have certain clarity on what it is that you'd like to manifest into your life, write it down in your journal in the form of a *positive statement* experienced in the *here and now.*

Again, make your statement very clear and easy to say.

Example One: I am experiencing abundance and wealth. Money is coming to me in wonderful and unexpected ways, which allows me more peace and joy in my life.

Example Two: I want more money. My bills are overwhelming, and I can't keep up. I'm tired of not having enough, and I don't want to be stressed about it anymore.

Which example do you think will more easily bring abundance? Imagine yourself saying both these statements. Which one gives you a positive, peaceful, confident feeling?

Yes, you're right. It's the first one.

The difference in these two examples is the wording. They both make a declaration for wanting more money and less stress, but example number one uses positive words with a positive tone. It is also making its statement in the here and now, not in the future. If your statement is pointing to the future, then you will always be waiting for your thoughts to manifest. The future is not now. You will never actually be in the future. Even when time goes by and the future comes, you will still be in the present. *You can never be in the future.* You are always physically in the here and now. Therefore, your statement must be constructed using the present tense.

Here's another example of positive wording in the present:

"I am now experiencing perfect health and all systems of my body are flourishing. I feel strong because I am strong. I am filled with vitality."

Or

"I am so healthy, I have boundless energy. I am aware of the healing light that flows in and around my body."

Both are great examples! Even if you don't currently have good health (or money, or a partner, or that perfect job, or joy, or your dream house, or a college acceptance letter, or _____ (fill in the blank)), *you must word your statement as if you already have it.*

Get very specific on what you want. If you simply want good health, the statements above are great. But if you want to stop getting

UTIs, create a statement that has more detail. (By the way, constant, recurring UTIs are a Sacral Chakra issue.)

Make all your verbs reflect the present. Never the future. An example of making the statement using the future tense is "I want to be healthy," or "I see myself becoming healthy."

Do not phrase what you are seeking for yourself from a negative perspective. "I see the sickness in me going away." Or (the double whammy) "I want to be free from this sickness" (negative and in the future). Remember, be very clear with yourself. What do you want? Do you want to be free from sickness or do you want boundless, great health?

Know that as soon as you make your positive statement, the wheels of energy start turning, and the Universe starts making the match. The vibrational frequency of what you want is being matched with more of that same frequency in the Universe. The more you focus on it, the more the Universe will match frequencies that line up with the thing you desire. As this continues, your thought form soon builds up with more and more energy until it can exist as a possibility on the level of physicality.

A word about great health. If you have been very sick for years and your body has suffered greatly, it will take time for it to heal. There may have been significant damage done to your body over the course of your life. To heal will require manifesting without doubt as well as deep meditation with your intentions focused on the blueprint of your body from the etheric layer of your auric field. It will also require nourishment in the form of energy and high vibrating foods, and the removal of toxins and low vibrating foods. Also, as you know, letting go of the emotions that led you to where you are regarding your health.

- Step 3. Close your eyes and say your positive statement aloud or with your inner voice. As you say your statement, visualize what it means.

If you are using the abundance example, you will want to see yourself enjoying life because now you have the time to relax. Visualize your bank account and see an incredible sum. See yourself very calmly opening your bills because you know you have plenty of money to pay them. You can even visualize treating yourself to something special because so much money is coming to you, and you deserve it. The emotional part of this visualization is important. You must *feel* the joy, peace, and freedom that comes with abundance. What does it feel like to have a lot of money? What kind of person are you when you have abundance? What does it feel like to have the freedom associated with wealth? Let yourself really feel it as you visualize and imagine.

- Step 4. *Never* let any doubt or negativity come into your mind.

Think of these two things as cancelers. They are the hot water on your snowball. They will slow down or put a stop to whatever it is you are trying to create. This negativity usually comes in one of two forms, and sometimes both.

1. Your own doubt. Doubting yourself or the outcome will destroy the thought form you have put into motion. If doubts do creep in, quickly dismiss them from your mind and go back to positive intention. The quicker you do this, the less damage you will have done to your work. Remember, there is no reason you should not have what you want. You were not singled out by some unseen power that declared you're the one who should suffer or go without! We are all equal players, and there is plenty of everything to go around for everyone. *All things are available to all of us.* If you want it, you may have it. Sometimes doubt can take root when you start wondering *how*. "How am I going to get myself millions of dollars?" Don't get bogged down in the how.

The Universe is limitless and can line itself up with your intentions. Think of it as a Rubik's Cube that the Universe and all of Spirit is lining up. You're all creating together. You will be in awe when your thoughts manifest on the physical plane in the most unique and unforeseen ways. (Or maybe you won't be in awe because you never doubted in the first place, right?)

2. Doubt, negative comments, and unsupportive behavior from friends, relatives, coworkers, and the media are the other cancelers. If these negative-thinking people find out what you are trying to accomplish, they will happily tell you every imaginable reason why you will fail. Stay clear of them! When they start to lecture you on why you'll never get what you want, change the subject, politely ask them to keep their thoughts to themselves, or just walk away! You don't need *their* negative outlook on *your* life to spoil *your* goals! Take a look at the state of their lives. Do they seem to have it all? Complete happiness? Confidence? Perfect relationships? Stockpiles of money? Probably not. These folks do not subscribe to the same beautiful, positive Universe full of possibilities as you do. Stick with like-minded people. People who do seem to have it all or people who share your way of thinking will support you every step of the way. If the media is broadcasting ideas that are opposite to what you want to create, turn off the TV, put down the newspaper. The media rarely touts positive vibes anyway.

If doubt does somehow find its way into your thoughts and you are having trouble getting them out of your head, the easiest way to put a stop to it is to just simply go to sleep. All of your negative thoughts will come to a stop, and when you wake up you can get right back to creating what you want. You can also do any of the activities listed in the Raise It Up! section in chapter three.

- Step 5. Do Your Part!
  - If you're trying to manifest good health but you won't stop eating fast food, there is a conflict there.
  - If you're trying to manifest a career as a singer but you've never performed publicly, there is a conflict there.
  - If you want to travel the world but you haven't researched the journey, there is a conflict there.
  - If you want happiness but you spend your time with very low-vibrating people, there is a conflict there.
  - If you want a lot of money but you don't seek opportunities, there is a conflict there.

Don't wait for things to happen to you. Be the artist of your own picture. Take action where you can! Where you can't, let the Law of Attraction take over and then co-create with the Universe. Remember, if you want something bad enough, make it happen. If you have already put your powerful and creative energy in motion, then you have done your job. The Universe, Source, and all of Spirit are your copilots and they want you to succeed. They want you to experience all the joy you desire. So let's go. Make it happen!

On a Personal Note

We *can* create what we want, you just have to realize you are a powerful creative energy being! Using powerful and creative thought I have manifested a happy life. Here are a few examples:

- Three different homes. I didn't have three homes simultaneously, but I bought three homes at different times in my life that were totally out of my reach for three different reasons. Through powerful and creative thought, I was able to purchase and live in each one. I started by creating a manifestation statement. I was very specific about how I wanted each home to look, inside and out. When the real estate agent told me I had no chance of getting the house, I was still certain I would live there. I imagined family gatherings, holidays, and birthdays in the house. While lying in bed at night, I visualized decorating and placing furniture. I started to imprint my energy into the energy of the house. When the manifestation became a reality, I wasn't surprised at all because I never let doubt into my mind. On the contrary, I would have been floored with disappointment if I didn't get these homes, because I always knew the outcome would be favorable to me.

- Seven-and-a-half-pound twins. I'm going to elaborate on this story because I really do like telling it. This was not a case of me not being able to conceive. It was a case of my former husband saying we would only have two children, my first child and the one I was pregnant with. He was calling all the shots. I desperately wanted three children, but it takes two to tango. Regardless, I kept envisioning three. I focused on three Souls that I wanted to have in my life. I didn't envision twins (since there had never been twins in my family), but I kept a focus on three. When I was five months pregnant, my doctor and I were aware of only one baby. It was time for my first ultrasound. The technician was taking much longer than I remembered from my first pregnancy. Finally, she spoke. Her exact words were, "How many babies are we here for? Because here's what I'm seeing." She pointed to the ultrasound monitor and said, "Here's Baby A and here's Baby B." I was overwhelmed with joy, and then worry set in. I had spent those five months treating this pregnancy as a singleton. I ate much less than I did the first time I was pregnant because I didn't want to gain those extra twenty-five pounds again. I ignored how tired I was all the time so I could keep up with my two-year-old daughter. I was stressed because my marriage was going downhill fast. I had two stays in the hospital because I developed a slew of kidney stones that I had to deal with while pregnant. My body (and the babies) suffered a lot of stress because of the stones and the deteriorating marriage, meaning tiny or premature babies were possible. I started manifesting healthy, big babies. I told my body over and over that I would not give birth to babies under five pounds. I thought about it, dreamed about it, talked about it. I employed everything I knew to create big healthy babies. Other than the kidney stones, I stayed healthy the whole time and carried them to term. Seven-and-a-half-pound babies are big, even for a single baby. I remember saying to my then husband who only wanted two babies, "Tell me what else I can't have." It was a snide comment for sure. But I knew it then and I know it now, I'm a powerful creator that cannot be stopped!

- A thriving business. After a rough divorce I was left with very little. My oldest was five and the twins were two. All the money I had was the money I earned at work that day. I had to create a successful business to be able to give my kids food and a home to live in. Failing was not an option for me. Of course, in the beginning, my clientele was very sparse. This was back in the days before social media was a thing and websites were not as popular as they are today. I spent money on one advertisement in a newspaper. The rest of my advertising time went into using powerful and creative energy in alliance with the Universe. When asked how my business was going, I spoke about it as if it was already thriving. I thought about what I knew I needed and wanted: a minimum of twenty clients per week who wanted to heal. I remember someone once commented to me that I was very brave to set out on my own. I didn't see it as bravery. I only recognized that failing was not an option. The only option left was success, so we made it happen. (By *we* I mean me, Source, Spirit, and the Universe.) Very quickly my business went from a couple of clients here and there to a waiting list.

Even when the economy slowed down, I was blessed with more than a full schedule for years.

- Healing. I healed myself from at least three serious physical ailments (one of which I was told by a surgeon would require shoulder surgery) by using the same principles. I focused on only one outcome. I did my part by changing my diet, adding natural remedies, and reducing stress. I visualized white light healing the areas that were out of balance. I meditated. I let go of emotional baggage. Every time I noticed a small improvement, I allowed myself to celebrate it as if it were a giant leap forward. I healed without westernized medicine or surgery. That type of healing worked for me because of who I am and the type of medicine I believe in. Other people will benefit more by incorporating westernized medicine into their healing process. You must do what works for you. Remember, there is never any judgment. Make smart choices for yourself and employ your power. I also healed a broken rib in three weeks by inviting in an abundance of healing white light. I walked away from Lyme disease by visualizing I was walking away from it, as well as reducing my stress level (divorce) tremendously. Stress is like a little monster inside of us looking to create as much destruction as possible. You have to learn to let it go. Just let it go.

The successes I listed above are some of my big ones. Day to day I have created other wonderful, fabulous things for myself. You just have to put in the effort, acknowledge the true essence of who you are, eliminate doubt, and know you are a wonderful, powerful energy being!

Believe It and Let Go!

Start living and behaving as if you have already achieved the thing you are trying to manifest. Allowing negative ideas or doubt to work its way into your mind will undo all the powerful thought you have already put into place. Have you ever heard the expression "You gotta walk the walk and talk the talk"? Well in this instance, that expression means you have to act, think, talk, and know in a way that lines up with the thought you are creating into physicality.

For example, if you desire abundance, you have to start behaving in a way that reflects that.

This does *not* mean you should spend every last penny you have because apparently you are about to come into mega-money.

This does *not* mean buying a Bentley when you should really be buying a Honda.

This does *not* mean spending your savings to go on a lavish, bougie vacation in Tahiti.

It does mean to stop focusing on and saying to anyone who will listen to you how much money you don't have. When a bill comes, do you usually think to yourself something like, *Oh geez, another bill! All these bills! I don't have enough money! How am I going to pay all these bills?* Or do you pass by some huge houses and think to yourself, *I'll never have enough money to live in one of those houses?* If you do, instead tell yourself, *Everything is okay. I am creating abundance in my life. I attract abundance naturally. It is my Soul-right to have all that I desire.*

Are you starting to see how these kinds of statements are similar to the thoughts needed for creating? When you say, "I don't have enough money to (FILL IN THE BLANK)" you are sending vibrations out to the Universe that match that statement. In turn, the Law of Attraction (and the Universe) are sending the same thing back to you, which, in this case, is not enough money. It's matching your thoughts.

Think about this statement: *Rich people are snobby.*

This is a limiting belief that can get passed down knowingly or unknowingly by a family member or friend.

If this is part of your belief system, and you believe that you yourself are not snobby, then how can you ever be rich? To be rich, would mean you would also be snobby, which you know you are not. Instead, let yourself understand that there are all kinds of rich people in the world. Some are rich and snobby, some are rich and kind, some are rich and altruistic, some are rich and stingy, some are rich and generous, some are rich and in debt, and so on and so on. Decide which type of rich person you would like to be because there are so many choices other than just rich and snobby. By letting go of that limiting belief, you are creating more probability of being successful in your manifestation. You will also be letting go of negative opinions, and the world will suddenly become a more positive, joyful place by your simple act of releasing one limiting belief.

The fundamentals of this example can be applied to almost any limiting belief. One of the best ways to let go of limiting beliefs that surround groups of people is to get to know those people on a deep and personal level.

Let's continue with the rich people example. Over the years, I have met many different types of fabulous, loving people, some of whom are very rich. To say rich people are snobby is not only very judgmental, but it is also lumping an entire group of people into one category without meeting every single wealthy individual from around the entire world. When we can get to know a person for who they actually are and not generalize based on what we think they are, people are almost always amazing, kind, quirky, friendly, interesting, unique, and fun to be with. If they aren't, you just haven't gotten to know them deeply enough yet. Try harder. You will find what you're looking for. How much more wonderful would the world be if we accepted people for the Love that shines through them rather than the stigma that somehow got attached to their demographic many years ago?

Limiting Belief Exercise

The following are questions that will help you realize your true feelings and limiting beliefs about love, health, money, race, religion, and gender. Try to answer these as truthfully as possible. You are the only one who will ever see the answers. After you answer the questions, look them over without judgment. Do the answers seem justified, accurate, positive? If you don't like your answers, are you willing to change?

Love

1. Love relationships are …

2. When you see others in a relationship you feel …

3. Your previous relationships were _____ and _____.

4. Your parents' relationship with each other is/was …

5. Some things that hold me back from being in a relationship (or closer to my partner) are …

6. What are your fears around being close with a partner?

7. What are some things a good relationship can provide?

8. How do you feel about being in a monogamous relationship?

9. What, if anything, would you be deprived of by being in a close, meaningful relationship?

10. Can a relationship work even if it has imperfections?

11. Can your love for your partner supersede problems within the relationship?

12. Make a list of your perfect mate's characteristics. Make the list as long or short as you like. (Use this to manifest the person you want.)

Health

1. Do you consider yourself to be in good health?

2. When you're not feeling well, how do your family/friends react to you?

3. What is your very first memory of being sick, and who took care of you?

4. Would you want that same person to take care of you now if you were sick?

5. In what ways do you benefit from being sick?

6. In what ways do you benefit from being well?

7. What would change in your life if you were completely healed today?

8. What immediate changes can you make to start feeling better?

9. Why have you not already made these changes?

10. Can you think of any good things that have come from your current health situation?

11. What is more important to you than your own good health?

Money

1. Money is …

2. People who have a lot of money (or no money) are …

3. What are your earliest memories of money?

4. What were your parents' views of money?

5. What do you enjoy about money?

6. What, if any, challenges do you have concerning money?

7. How do you feel when you think about or talk to others about money?

8. Do you view money as useful, the enemy, or both?

9. What does money allow you to do, or keep you from doing?

10. You have $10 million. What are you going to do with it?

11. How do you feel when you are in a room with others who have much more money than you? Much less money than you?

Race/Religion/Gender

1. Are you thankful you were born the race that you are? Why?

Religion?

Gender?

2. Do you notice inequalities placed on other races?

Religions?

Genders?

3. Are you interested in learning about traditions or needs of other races?

Religions?

Genders?

4. Have you ever played a part (no matter how big or small) in a situation that caused someone to experience hardship because of their race?

Religion?

Gender?

5. Do you quietly judge others in the private recesses of your mind based on their race?

Religion?

Gender?

6. Would members of your family be opposed to you being romantically involved with someone from a different race?

Religion?

Same Gender?

7. If there were only two seats left in a room, one next to someone who looked just like you and one next to someone of a race you have had limited interaction with, which seat would you pick?

Religion?

Gender?

8. Do you accept that people of a different race are just like you on a Soul level?

Religion?

Gender?

TWELVE

THE LITTLE CAR AND YOUR BODY

How Far Can Your Car Go?

As you read this, keep in mind our premise that Soul is to body as human is to car.

You have planned a road trip to go across the country, and you're so excited! You have a destination in mind, but really you know you planned this trip because of the journey and all the wonderful experiences you're sure to have along the way. New sights to see, interesting people to meet, and the feeling of freedom on the open road. Oh my!

After you pack the car, you pull it out of the garage, down the driveway, and off you go! About halfway into your journey, you start to hear a clunking sound coming from the right side of your little car. You become slightly concerned, but you decide to ignore it. Soon the clunking gets louder. Then you remember you haven't changed the oil in over two years, and when you did change it, you used the cheapest brand you could find. Clunk, clunk, clunk! Oh dear! As you go up the hills your little car seems to be gasping for air as other cars fly past you. You push down harder on the gas pedal, only to see the temperature gauge light up. What's happening to your little car? Miraculously, you make it to the top of the hill.

And now you're coasting downhill. Everything seems to have quieted for the moment. You choose not to look at your flashing gauges because you assume what you don't know can't hurt you. At the bottom of the hill is a huge sign for a service station five miles away. A voice in your head strongly suggests you stop and figure out what's wrong with the little car, but the next sign says "McDonald's" and you think to yourself *Woo-hoo! That sounds good!* After sucking down a milkshake you get back in the driver's seat. The little car seems to be in bad shape. It starts up, but there's steam coming out of the hood, the clunking sound has turned into a banging noise, and there's black soot coming out of the tailpipe. Time to call a tow truck! The little car is sick and needs to spend some time at the service station. Sadly, you need to put the road trip on hold.

You're keeping in mind that the little car represents your body, and you are your Soul, right?

We have talked a lot about the Soul and the amazing journey it wants to have. But the body needs to be taken care of just like a car needs care, because when the body stops being able to take you (Soul) on the journey, your experiences will certainly change from what was originally intended. Nurturing the body by eating right, exercising, and eliminating harmful products are as important as nurturing the spiritual experience.

The American diet, also called the SAD diet (Standard American Diet) is known as one of the worst diets in the world. Our food and personal care products are crafted and processed in a lab. Many foods are made into something that looks like food, but they don't come from the same quality ingredients our grandparents ate. They're laced with pesticides, herbicides, GMO's, hormones, hormone disruptors, carcinogens, toxins, and other unsafe ingredients. On the shelves of American stores there are many personal care products that have ingredients outlawed by European countries because they are too dangerous for the human body.

According to the Centers for Disease Control and Prevention (CDC) an unhealthy diet contributes to serious diseases like type 2 diabetes, heart disease, some cancers, stroke, menstrual and menopause problems, hypertension, and digestive disorders. It is also known that poor diet can lead to allergies, premature aging, dental complications, high cholesterol, muscle pain, liver problems, reproductive issues, etc. But eating holistically, organically, and healthily are luxuries that are not affordable to every American.

There is a severe imbalance when it comes to which Americans get to eat great food and which Americans have to eat the food they can afford. This is something that needs to be addressed. But until then, here are some ways to get more wholesome food into your refrigerator. (Remember, if you want something bad enough, you can manifest it into your reality.)

- Try going vegetarian. This will greatly cut down your food bill and protect your body from dangerous substances that Big Ag puts into your meat like chlorine, ammonia, carbon monoxide, bacteriophages, sodium tripolyphosphate (EcoWatch 2014).
- Get on the internet and educate yourself about the dangerous ingredients found in processed foods. Then read labels while you're at the grocery store. Pick better alternatives to the very toxic, processed foods.
- Choose single-ingredient foods (or close to single-ingredient foods).
- Grow a garden. You have choices here. If you have the space, grow a traditional garden. If you don't, vertical gardens, community gardens, and indoor gardens are options. Big pots can also work well on a small deck or terrace.
- Keep track of how much sugar you eat. According to the American Heart Association, women should have no more than six teaspoons per day (twenty-four grams) and men should have no more than nine teaspoons per day (thirty-six grams). Children between the ages of two and eighteen should consume no more than nineteen grams per day. That's less than four teaspoons. According to the American Heart Association, the average child actually consumes about eighty-one grams of sugar per day. That means added sugars. It does not include sugar from carbohydrates and fruits. Sugar is also found in almost every processed food. Read the labels! You will find added sugar in things like

yogurt, cereal, power bars, juice and other drinks, pickles, ketchup, peanut butter, salad dressing, tomato sauce, cured meats, bread, soup, etc. It is also important to realize there are between fifty-six and seventy-five different names for sugar (depending on what list you look at) that food manufactures are allowed to use in the ingredients. Research and get to know these names so you can spot them on labels. Track how many grams of sugar you eat in a day. Does it exceed the recommended amount? (Keep in mind, the American SAD diet is sad for a reason. Are six and nine teaspoons too much?) According to Harvard Health Publishing, Harvard Medical School (2022) too much sugar will cause high blood pressure, inflammation, weight gain, diabetes, fatty liver disease, etc. Chronic low-grade inflammation will cause cancer, cardiovascular disease, and others health problems. (Inflammation can also come from stress. Stress is a product of an emotional event perceived negatively.)

- As you educate yourself about food, you will start to make better choices around which foods you will accept as quality, and which you know are not suitable to sustain great health. A health coach can help if this seems overwhelming, but much of what you need to know to start your healthy eating journey can be found on the internet, podcasts, or in books.

- As you start to understand your Chakras, you may begin to notice where your emotions are buried. Are you using food to pacify pain from an experience? Are your emotions making you feel void of Love? Do you feel like you may be trying to fill that void with food? Getting in touch with a good eating disorder therapist and a health coach may be your first best steps.

- Your skin is very efficient at absorbing topical chemicals into the body. If you've ever used hormone creams, a patch for nicotine or hormones, and essential oils, you're well aware of how effectively this works. The skin will also absorb unwanted ingredients in personal care products that are used every day. Many of them are hormone disruptors. If you are having fertility or reproductive issues, consider using natural personal care products. Endocrine disruptors will challenge your reproductive organs. Look at the ingredients of the creams and shampoos you use daily. Do they contain any of the following?

- Parabens (disrupt hormones and negatively affects fertility)
- Sodium lauryl sulfate (carcinogen and endocrine disruptor)
- 1,4-Dioxane (human carcinogen and toxic to organs)
- Triclosan (changes thyroid function and disrupts endocrine function)
- Formaldehyde (human carcinogen and respiratory toxin)
- Phthalates and DEHP (damage to nervous and reproductive systems, liver, kidneys, and lungs)
- Benzophenone and styrene (endocrine disruptors)

To find product lists and their toxicity levels, check out the websites Cosmily or EWG's Skin Deep Cosmetics Database (EWG has a great app that can make shopping for food and personal products easier. Just scan the barcode and it will pull up the product you are considering). These two websites will explain the dangers of each ingredient in your product and rate its toxicity level in order to provide as much transparency as possible. EWG's website offers a little extra help by showing you similar products you can replace your toxic product with.

Like the little car, we need to take care of our body, inside and out, so our Soul can have the amazing adventure it signed up for. The human experience is meant for the Soul, but it cannot be done without the successful functioning of the body.

So pay attention to your Chakras, your Soul Goals, shed limiting beliefs, and start to know yourself as the beautiful, powerful being that you are. You are a Soul! Go ahead and decorate that body of yours if you like, have fun with it and use it to express who you feel you are as a Soul. Just remember, you are a powerful and creative energy being and you're here to experience as much as you can! But also keep your body healthy and make sure it sparkles on the inside. It's the only one you've got (this lifetime).

GLOSSARY OF KEY TERMS

This glossary is here for you to thumb through as your reading if you need help understanding important concepts of spirituality, or you can read it through before you start chapter one. *Each of these concepts is discussed in greater detail as you journey through the book.*

For many people, the information that follows is completely new. Some of these words are used in every day conversations, but here they may have a different meaning. So this section is dedicated to simply giving you definitions of our most important words and concepts.

1. *Angels.* There are many orders of Angels. Archangels have specific jobs like helping to heal and protect, watching over children or animals, assisting in creativity or relationships, and many others. Guardian Angels are assigned to your Soul and have been with you since your beginning. Your Guardian Angel loves you unconditionally and is *always* with you, even when you feel alone—so you are *never* actually alone. Angels want to help us in any way they can. But because humans have free will, they cannot interfere with our lives unless we specifically ask for their help. Once we clearly ask for help, they are eager to do all they can that is in our highest and best interest. Sometimes it may seem that our plea for help goes unanswered, which can reinforce that feeling of being very alone. From our human perspective, it is very difficult to see the best plan we have in place for ourselves. The big picture is unseen. Our Angels, however, do see the big picture and can more easily see what is in our highest and best interest. If you're asking for help in regards to getting that job but then you don't get it, or if you're asking for help mending a love relationship and the relationship continues to go downhill, it is possible these things are not in

your highest and best interest. The job could, years later, lead you to a dead end. The relationship, if mended, could hold you back from meeting someone better suited for you. These are just a few examples of how we cannot see the big picture that exists in the future. There are many other examples, most of which are very sophisticated. But remember, Angels are always around us. They are constantly sending us love and love us unconditionally. Remember that! They love us unconditionally.

2. *Energy.* The creative, positive force that comes from Source and the Universe. When you understand energy, you can create, or change, or be anything! Energy can be Love Energy, Healing Energy, or Creative Energy. Negative energy also exists but does not come from Source. Negative energy comes from an experience that the individual perceives as not good, unwanted, harmful, distasteful, disastrous, unkind, non-beneficial, hateful, etc. When an expectation is not met, the experience is felt as negative. In reality, the experience is neutral. It is only our subjective interpretation of the thing or event that assigns a negative or positive energy to it. As individuals and as a society we have, over the years, assigned positivity and negativity to almost all aspects of life. Sometimes thoughts evolve enough to change the energy around an experience. Fashion is a fantastic yet basic example of this. Look at pictures from the 1970s and you'll see short shorts on professional basketball players, bell-bottom pants, oversized collars, and the worst of all, corduroy suits. Very in vogue styles at the time. Not so much in style by the mid-to-late '80s, though. The energy changes rather quickly regarding fashion.

When a negative thought gains enough momentum, negative energy can have devastating power. The momentum of negative energy can fill a person, a room, an institution, a coalition, a way of life, a society.

There are only two "bookends" of energy. They are Love and Fear. Everything in the Universe comes from one of these two energies. Some may think that hate is the opposite end of Love and deserves to be a bookend, but it is not the initial, originating energy. Hate comes out of Fear. The only reason a person will bring the emotional energy of hate into his awareness is because he initially had Fear. Hate is born from Fear. Hate can also be taught, but its origins come from Fear. *Fear Energy* comes from your own subjective understanding of an event. How you construe and interpret it will create the Fear Energy. In reality, the event is neutral. Because we are human with human instincts, some events need to be interpreted as fearful. For example, the fear activated when being confronted by a predator is good and necessary because it will activate the next necessary reactions, which are to flee, fight back, or outwit. In our history, we can recall events that unnecessarily activated fear, like meeting a person different from ourselves, although they were not predators. Let's use the LGBTQ+ community and the heterosexual community as an example. Though there are degrees of differences between these two groups, there is no threat. Unfortunately, in our history, the differences activated fear for some (not all) individuals or groups, and the Fear Energy, needing an outlet, morphed into hate. At that moment a limiting belief was born.

Here is another example. A man showers a woman he has just met with adoration, attention, and affection. These are emotions that are born out of Love Energy. The woman, unfortunately for the man, has no reciprocating affection. In fact, she is quite put off by it and finds his advances toward her undesirable. The energy being put forth by the man comes from Love Energy, but the woman is perceiving it as negative. The Love Energy came to her awareness in neutral form, but she has chosen to perceive it as negative energy.

Love Energy originates from Source and we use it in many different capacities. Love Energy can sometimes be confused with the emotion of love. The idea of love in an emotional context is a feeling or an expression of how we feel about someone or something else. In a spiritual context, Love is the highest vibrational frequency of all and is used as a noun rather than a verb (or emotion). Love is an energy that comes from Source and is used by all beings, including humans, to create beauty and goodness in the Universe and in our lives. It is an energy from which all other high-vibrating frequencies are born—joy, happiness, forgiveness, confidence, creativity, open-mindedness, truth, compassion, kindness, peace, etc. Hate is a very low-vibrating frequency, but it is not the dynamic opposite of Love. The opposite is Fear Energy. Hate is the lowest-vibrating frequency that comes out of Fear.

3. *Energy field or auric field.* Your own personal energy field around your physical body and is unique to you. There are multiple bodies of energy that make up the auric field, each one in relationship with the Chakra system. The one easiest to discern is of course, the physical body. The next four are the etheric body, emotional body, mental body, and spiritual body.

4. *Law of Attraction.* "Like attracts like" is the most basic concept of this law. Using intention, you can project thoughts out into the Universe, and any energy or vibrational frequency that matches it will come back to you. Thoughts are energy that hold a vibrational frequency. When that vibration finds a match in the Universe, the match will then build its momentum and allow you to create. Law of Attraction works with both positive and negative thoughts. The type of energy you project out from yourself is equal to what will be attracted back to you. Know that if you immerse yourself and your thoughts in that which is positive and that which vibrates at a high rate, then

positive, high-vibrating things will be easily found on your path through life. If you do the opposite and immerse yourself and your thoughts in that which is negative and vibrates at a low frequency, you will find a very negative, low-vibrating path in front of you. Meaning, your experiences and feelings will have a more negative result. Continuously focusing on one very clear idea for an extended period activates the Law of Attraction and causes a manifestation. Law of Attraction requires the Universe to provide to us that which we clearly focus on, good or bad. This concept is very basic and clear, yet so hard for most of us to one hundred percent subscribe to, usually because of limiting beliefs.

5. *Limiting beliefs.* These are foundational beliefs that we have acquired from our parents, family, ancestors, teachers, political and religious leaders, and even past lives. We as individuals do not question these beliefs. They are something we just simply weave into the fabric of our beings as children, and as we mature we are unaware of how these beliefs hold us back from success and happiness. We can also create new limiting beliefs in addition to those we learned from our elders. Recognizing these beliefs and releasing them from our consciousness can be a lifelong journey or can be immediate. It is our choice. Holding on to them can cause constraints and perpetuate negative energy within a person, group, institution, culture, or society. Limiting beliefs can halt manifestations.

6. *Powerful and Creative Energy.* When you create with thought, you are using Law of Attraction. Energy follows thought. When you think about something over and over, the vibrational frequencies of that thought attracts Energy from the Universe. In time, this Energy will manifest into physical form.

7. *Soul.* The true essence of who you are. Your Soul (which is you) is a piece of Source. Your Soul is the light within you that is Source. The analogy "If you take a drop of water from the sea, is it just water, or is it a part of the sea?" is used to explain the relationship between Soul and Source. We are many Souls, and we are all a part of Source. If you take many drops from the sea, are they individual drops of water, or are they all a part of the same sea? If you pour them back into the sea, do they remain separate from each other and from the sea, or have they all merged back as one to be a part of the great sea?

   Our consciousness within our being is unique and bridges Soul to body. That bridge can be thought of as the mind.

8. *Source.* Also known as God, Goddess, The Creator, Divine Energy, The All, and Great Spirit. It is that which is greater than yourself. When you read about Source in this book, you may find yourself connecting with the God taught in religions. If this is your preference, this is completely acceptable. If you do not subscribe to a religion, you should understand that the Source Energy you read about in this book is that which consists of all Love, all good, all knowing, all healing, all that is perfect. It is not necessary to have a background in religion to understand or connect with Source. Source is not to be feared or perceived as unapproachable, rather just the opposite! Source is the birthplace of our Souls, as well as the nucleus of Love Energy.

9. *Spirit.* The word Spirit refers to both a "place" as well as a group of higher beings. Spirit can be very loosely compared to heaven in that it is the "place" Souls exist before they enter and after they leave their bodies. It is also the space where higher beings reside. Higher beings consist of Angels, Archangels, Guardian Angels, Spirit Guides, higher self, ascended masters, Source

Energy, and more. The word Spirit can be used interchangeably when speaking about a place or about higher beings.

10. *Spirit Guides.* These are Souls who have lived on the earth (usually for many lifetimes) and have acquired enough wisdom to become a Spirit Guide. When we decide to incarnate, we are assigned a minimum of one, but usually two or more, Spirit Guides who will stay with us through our lifetime or through cycles of our lives. We may have a Spirit Guide for our personal life and another one for our professional life. As we move forward from one phase of life to another, the Spirit Guide residing with us may leave, and another one more suited for that phase of our life moves in. Before Souls can become Spirit Guides, they must go through rigorous "training" that will prepare them to be wise, insightful, and helpful guides. Unlike Angels, Spirit Guides can intercede for the betterment of our lives. They will try turning our attention in certain directions, place signs on our path, etc. They will also try to guide us in a direction that enables us to have our chosen experiences, but with as little suffering or no suffering on our part as possible. But it is still up to us to take notice of the help and guidance they are offering. If we are not aware, these signs will go unnoticed, and opportunities will remain untaken. We are not meant to navigate this life on our own. Life can be tricky, and we have a whole gang of helpers who love us and want to help us succeed. Spirit Guides stay in the form of energy and help us indirectly. When we learn to be more aware of who we are beyond our physical body, it becomes so much easier to tune in to the help, guidance, and support they are constantly offering to us.

11. *Spirituality.* This is an awareness of an infinite presence that encompasses all that is good. Spirituality recognizes we are more than physical beings. Rather, we are energy beings enjoying a physical existence in a physical dimension. Spirituality can

be thought of as a lifestyle and a way of conducting ourselves while we exist on the planet. Love, oneness, transcendence, and awakening are cornerstones of the enlightened concept of spirituality.

12. *Universal Energy Field (UEF).* A plasma of energy that is all around us and is the place that contains limitless information for our use. When you raise your vibrational frequency to match a frequency in the UEF, it's like unlocking a door that holds information for clarity and ingredients to create. As you grow spiritually, you graduate to new levels in this energy field. It's as if you are given a new key to unlock a new door. Your vibrational energy starts to match vibrations in this field, and you become more and more enlightened. If you're not ready to unlock a new door (physically, mentally, emotionally, or spiritually), these frequencies will not be in your awareness and therefore will not be available to you.

13. *Universe.* The Universe, in scientific terms, is the endless space that contains galaxies, solar systems, black holes, suns, etc. The Universe, in terms of spirituality, is this same endless space, but even more. It is the platform that contains the building blocks to anything we desire. The Universe is vast and unexplored, maybe even unexplorable. But within it are the raw ingredients in the form of energy that are necessary to create. Anything and everything we wish to manifest or create comes from the quarry of energy provided by the Universe (which does ultimately originate with Source). Think of the Universe as a vast and endless warehouse. Inside the warehouse is every conceivable thing you could ever need. Imagine if the wholesale stores Costco and BJ's, Wegmans, Whole Foods, Walmart, Target, Dick's, and every outlet store in the world put everything they sold into one warehouse. All you will ever need in one place. The Universe holds within it everything you will ever need, and it is

in the form of energy. Remember, everything starts off as energy. Everything *is* energy. The Universe holds within in it all that you desire. When you understand who you are beyond your physical body, you will start to understand how easy it is to create from the endless supply given by the Universe.

14. *Vibrational energy (high).* This is energy that vibrates at a very high frequency. It includes anything that resonates on the positive side of the scale like Love (and all things born from Love like joy, happiness, selflessness, peace, forgiveness, confidence, hope, acceptance, respect, honesty, beauty, faith, trust, gratitude, etc.), dancing, singing, nature, laughing, creating, meditation, nutritious food, water, etc. The higher your vibrational frequency, the more wonderful you feel physically, emotionally, mentally, and spiritually. You experience greater personal power and clarity and creating becomes very easy. Raising your vibrational frequency can allow for a good connection with your Spirit Guides, Angels, Source and even loved ones who are in Spirit.

15. *Vibrational energy (low).* This is energy that vibrates at a very low frequency. Objects in physicality vibrate slowly but are not necessarily "low-vibrating." Anything that resonates on the negative side of the scale would be low-vibrating energy. Examples are Fear and all things born from Fear like hatred, jealousy, discrimination, resentment, hostility, disrespect, indifference, and animosity. Abusing drugs, alcohol, and tobacco will cause your energy being to vibrate at a lower level as well. Consuming processed foods, sugar, and inhumanly processed meat will also lower vibrational frequency.

Those who partake in the *occasional* use of earth-made hallucinogenics tend to not lower their vibrational frequency. In fact, some hallucinogens might even raise human vibration. Some say this leads to a heightened spiritual experience.

Laboratory-made recreational drugs, on the other hand, have a lowering effect on people from a vibratory standpoint. Whether it's natural or man-made, many people claim to need or want to use drugs to attain a euphoric experience. While there is no doubt something is altered when under the influence of substances, is it *necessary* to use drugs to find bliss? To fully harness bliss, it must come from within. Artificially induced bliss by way of outside sources is temporary and uncontrolled, especially in the case of individuals who use drugs to escape mental or emotional pain. When the drug wears off, the sense of euphoria will also wear off. If joy is not within your reach without drugs, it will not be within your reach with them. When we allow a peaceful flow of Love Energy into our beings, natural bliss will easily follow, but it's a matter of choice. Choose Love Energy and let go of painful emotions. When you can do this, you will feel a natural high that lets you ride on a constant cloud of bliss, bringing you to the highest level of spiritual awareness.

Those who occasionally consume things like alcohol, tobacco, drugs, and low-quality meat will not do permanent harm to their being. They have only introduced low vibrations into their energy field. Done consistently, and without replenishing positive energy, this can yield a very low-vibrating energy field. When a substance is abused or overused, the energy of that substance will overwhelm the human energy system, and it can become compromised. This is why we can physically feel lousy after overindulgence or spending a lot of time in fear-based emotions. If you do partake in lower vibrating activities or foods, just replenish with high-vibrating activities! Abuse of any substance, however, will require more spiritual work.

16. *Visualizing with the mind's eye.* During guided meditations to balance Chakras, you may be asked to visualize a color or your body being filled with white light. Some people feel concerned because they cannot see the colors being suggested to them. You

must realize the request to visualize is not about *seeing* the color or image. It is about bringing the frequency of that energy into your awareness. Do the following exercise with a friend and have them read this to you: *Close your eyes and think of: Blue truck. Black dog. Red apple. Old man. Small baby. Round white moon. Beautiful orange sunset. Blue Throat Chakra. White Light filling your body.* Could you see these things? Maybe, maybe not. But you definitely had an awareness of them. You were able to connect with the idea of each one. Whether you actually saw it is irrelevant. Bringing it into your awareness is what is important. By simply doing this, you are successfully connecting with the color or image. That's all that is necessary when visualizing with your mind's eye.

Ready to start your spiritual journey?

Go to www.mindfulbodywithsoul/meditations to listen to free guided meditations.

- Powerful Creative Energy Meditation
- Relax and Raise Vibe Meditation
- Chakra and Angel Meditation

Printed in the United States
by Baker & Taylor Publisher Services